Selected Poems

This eccentric and iconoclastic poet, born in Roumania in 1912, has lived in Canada since he was one year old and has spent the last 25 years teaching literature and history. Although he published his first volume of poems in 1945 (and has subsequently published some further 24 volumes) it was not until the mid 1950's that the critics began to take notice of him. But, having once attracted some favourable critical attention, his fortunes soared and by the mid 1960's he had acquired a considerable notoriety both for his poetry and for the controversial opinions he expressed in the press, on radio and television, and on reading and lecture tours.

Irving Layton's work is difficult to characterise—it is crude, erotic, provocative and uncontrollably versatile, but it is witty, evocative and often passionately lyrical too and the angry aggression of his work never obscures the joyful celebration of life, love and sex that pervades all his poetry. The very accessible nature of his work gives it an instant and irresistible appeal which perhaps belies the enduring quality of so much of his writing.

Selected Poems

Selected Poems

IRVING LAYTON

Edited with a preface by Wynne Francis

CHARISMA BOOKS LONDON

First published in Great Britain in 1974
Charisma Books are published by
Spice Box Books Ltd., 37 Soho Square, London W.1
Editorial offices: 70 Old Compton Street, London W.1

ISBN 085947 005 9

Printed in Great Britain by litho by
Anchor Press and bound by Wm. Brendon,
both of Tiptree, Essex

CONTENTS

PREFACE

by *Wynne Francis*

Irving Layton was born in Roumania in 1912 but
he has lived in Canada – mainly in Montreal – since
he was one year old. He holds a Bachelor of Science
degree in Agriculture and Economics (Macdonald
College 1939) and a Master's in Economics and
Political Science (McGill 1946). Between 1945 and
1960 he published twelve volumes of poems which won
for him, in spite of the antipathy or indifference of
most reviewers, a growing number of enthusiastic
readers. His first collection of poems (*The Improved
Binoculars,* Jonathan Williams, 1956) attracted some
favourable critical attention and thereafter Layton's
literary fortunes began to soar. His second collection
(*A Red Carpet for the Sun,* McClelland and Stewart,
1959) won the Governor-General's Award. Since then
he has published six more volumes including a third
Collected Poems (McClelland and Stewart, 1965).
His most recent publication *The Shattered Plinths*
(McClelland and Stewart, 1968) makes a total of
twenty volumes of poetry to date.

Layton has taught literature and history in the sec-
ondary schools and in the university during the past
twenty-five years. In 1966 he held the post of Poet in
Residence at Sir George Williams University in Montreal. Throughout the Sixties he became widely known
both for his poetry and for the controversial opinions
he expressed in the press, on radio and television, and
on reading and lecture tours in Canada and the United
States. Currently he is travelling in Europe and the
Orient.

Many Canadian readers in the Forties and Fifties

were repelled by the crude invective and frank eroticism in Layton's work. Even in the Sixties most reviewers were so preoccupied with the sensational aspects of his poetry that they failed to give adequate attention to its other important elements. This is partly Layton's own fault. A prolific writer, he proved to be an indiscriminate editor. Most of his volumes to date have included an inordinate number of ephemeral and inflammatory pieces. Moreover, he has frequently indulged in prefatory essays intended, no doubt, to throw light on his poems. These Forewords, however, were written in such a shrill and provocative style that they served mainly as reviewer-bait and distracted many a reader from taking the poems seriously.

Critics hardy enough to resist these distractions found themselves faced with other hurdles. Layton's versatility – what has been called the protean nature of his talent – has discouraged most critics from attempting an over-all view of his work. And since at the age of fifty-six Layton shows no signs of a lagging productivity, a measure of reluctance to begin an assessment of his prolific output is understandable. Nevertheless his best work to date deserves more critical consideration than it has so far received.

It is hoped that this present selection will serve to focus attention on some of the more enduring of Layton's poems. The arrangement is chronological and the poems have been chosen to reflect both the poet's broad stylistic spectrum and his most frequently recurring themes. Such an arrangement makes clear, for example, that even in the early books eroticism and invective were only two of the many facets of Layton's work – he is equally at ease in other modes such as the lyric, the satiric, the fantastic, and the prophetic. Furthermore, though a versatile stylist able to command and to freely adapt a variety of traditional forms,

Layton has stamped his signature, marked by passionate intensity, strong rhythms, and rhetorical flourish, on even his earliest poems. Lastly, it is apparent that no matter what mask he assumes – satyr, prophet, tender husband, jealous lover, teacher, father, minstrel, clown – Layton has been preoccupied with certain constantly recurring themes: the celebration of life in terms of love and sex; the denunciation of evil and corruption; compassion for the weak, the aged, the crippled; contemplation of death and of the mutability of youth and beauty; and an anguished recognition of the sacrifice and pain incurred by the inexorable process of nature and history. To these early and sustained themes may be added his growing conviction concerning the redemptive power of imagination and the prophetic role of the poet in society. All of these themes were explicit in his poetry by the mid-Fifties; his progression since then has been marked by deeper probings of his experience in these terms.

It will also be obvious from this selection that Layton's poetry is not easy to categorize. His eclecticism has led critics to see in his work the moral fervour of the Hebrew prophets, the ecstatic frenzy of a Dionysian reveller, the witty and joyous eroticism of Catullus, the visionary fire of Blake, the egotistic wilfulness of Byron, the barbaric yawp of Whitman, the anguished self-irony of Yeats, the rage and scorn of Pound. Something of each of these can indeed be found in various of Layton's poems; but it is the common denominator, passion – with its connotation of both suffering and joy – that is most characteristic of his work.

This quality of passion is a valuable clue to Layton's vision of reality. He is profoundly convinced of the positive existence of evil as a force dominating the world. Man is always at the mercy of the inhuman forces of nature and of the irreversible processes of history; but far worse, man as a moral being has created his own hell on earth. That this evil which man has created grows daily more real and horrible is attested to by the cruelty, violence, and hatred rampant in the world. All men are doomed to suffer. Yet the struggle of each individual – while it lasts – can have dignity if it is accepted with passion and delight. A man can even transform his defeat into a personal triumph with redemptive value for his fellow sufferers by affirming his power to love and his joy in the gift of imagination.

Layton's own suffering rage and defiant exultation suffuse all his poetry, but they are perhaps most cryptically rendered in these prophetic lines from a poem which he wrote in mid-career:

They dance best who dance with desire,
Who lifting feet of fire from fire
Weave before they lie down
A red carpet for the sun.

For Leonard Cohen and A. M. Klein

THE SWIMMER

The afternoon foreclosing, see
The swimmer plunges from his raft,
Opening the spray corollas by his act of war –
The snake heads strike
Quickly and are silent.

Emerging see how for a moment
A brown weed with marvellous bulbs,
He lies imminent upon the water
While light and sound come with a sharp passion
From the gonad sea around the Poles
And break in bright cockle-shells about his ears.

He dives, floats, goes under like a thief
Where his blood sings to the tiger shadows
In the scentless greenery that leads him home,
A male salmon down fretted stairways
Through underwater slums . . .

Stunned by the memory of lost gills
He frames gestures of self-absorption
Upon the skull-like beach;
Observes with instigated eyes
The sun that empties itself upon the water,
And the last wave romping in
To throw its boyhood on the marble sand.

DE BULLION STREET

Below this broad street inverted bell-jars
Hanging from wooden crucifixes drop
Tiny moons upon the shaven asphalt;
Rouged whores lean lips to narrow slits: they stop
The young soldier with his bag of salt.

Under the night's carapace, the soft lanes
Are listening ears where sudden footfall
Starts a choir of echoes. A red light winks
Viciously; and the wind's occasional
Sight lifts from the garbage pails their stinks.

Here private lust is public gain and shame;
Here the Oriental and the skipjack go;
Where those bleak outposts of the virtuous
The corner mission and the walled church grow
Like hæmorrhoids on the city's anus.

O reptilian street whose scaly limbs
Are crooked stairways and the grocery store,
Isolate, is your dreaming half-shut eye:
Each virgin at the barricaded door
Feels your tongue-kiss like a butterfly.

MORTUARY

Flesh has fallen away. Trees
And buildings are summer's skeleton;
Wind has loosened, disarrayed
The separate ribs, the evidence of bone.
Dead, deposited relics
Shored up clean against a stiffened sky,
Fixed by the mortician cold
Moving his fingers over them ceaselessly;
While the snow, decently to inter,
Drifts in between the spaces, everywhere.

NEWSBOY

Neither tribal nor trivial he shouts
From the city's centre where tramcars move
Like stained bacilli across the eyeballs,
Where people spore in composite buildings
From their protective gelatine of doubts,
Old ills, and incapacity to love
While he, a Joshua before their walls,
Sells newspapers to the gods and geldings.

Intrusive as a collision, he is
The Zeitgeist's too public interpreter,
A voice multiplex and democratic,
The people's voice or the monopolists';
Who with last-edition omniscience
Plays Clotho to each gaping customer
With halcyon colt, sex crime in an attic,
The story of a twice-jailed bigamist.

For him the mitred cardinals sweat in
Conclaves domed; the spy is shot. Empiric;
And obstreperous confidant of kings,
Rude despiser of the anonymous,
Danubes of blood wash up his bulletins
While he domesticates disaster like
A wheat in pampas of prescriptive things
With cries animal and ambiguous.

His dialectics will assault the brain,
Contrive men to voyages or murder,
Dip the periscope of their public lives
To the green levels of acidic caves;
Fever their health, or heal them with ruin,
Or with lies dangerous as a letter;
Finally enfold the season's cloves,
Cover a somnolent face on Sundays.

COMPLIMENTS OF THE SEASON

Returning with an annual passion
April winds suck buds, blow
Greenness into the palmate leaf and find
A passionate lady at dresser moulting.
Hair and cuticle stream with the season
Through her mirror.

Under the foraging sunlight
Humans rancid beside sweet-smelling trees
Sprawl between the thorns while Mount Royal
Slopes its green arms under their arses;
And the one-armed beggar
Brutal with red and yellow pencils
Dies with a windmill in his arms –
There were no shebas, not even jills.

At the base hospital behind the lines
Ideologies are carried out in bedpans;
And next april and the april after
The veterans of the two last wars
Will lay their crutches
Against the lighted cross
That shines steadfast upon the city
With the faith of its shareholders.

Against the curbstones like thick nostrils
The sunlight begins to dry
This snotflecked world.

THE YARD

No one prospers outside my door:
I sit like the first criminal with an old woman,
Her hair timesoaped her hands folded
Like a hymnal. Here everyone is dying out a pain.
I spy from my restricted gallery, a turret.

Outside my door everything is prepared:
From wooden scarps the clotheslines arch like scimitars,
The windingsheets swell under a bolshevik moon;
This evening the yard is full of fatal actors
Waiting with their garbage pails for the blue corpses.

Outside my door no one prospers:
The crumbling shards multiplying like flowers,
Tomorrow the casual stroke of a dirty urchin leg
Will prod the fire from them, a marathon blaze;
Later the cold-eyed men will infect the weather.

A column of whispers rises from the summermoist yard:
I think it is the neanderthal
Tree of Eden lifting its immense branches
Over my banisters for manslayer and saint;
And I am neither I am neuter I am you.

KARL MARX

They most dear, the sad-eyed astronomers,
The unprevailing princes who broke and fled;
Or Calvin, his golden beard full of the virtues,
And Luther who in a panic maimed a devil
Later repented caught and flogged a peasant –
The Moor has tidied their bones with a newspaper.

Now the winds are lashed howling to the Poles
And these bones charged with lightning
While his secular horse,
The shadow removed like a halter,
Moves magisterially into the sun;
And O you black ugly beast O my beauty
Churn up these white fields of leprosy!

PROOF READER

I whose eyes are a transmission belt,
The words depositing like strips of steel,
Think Cyclops luckier in his wounded cave:
Death comes for brothers like Bela Lugosi,
My brothers dying in a Roman hedge;
Their ache is frozen into proper type
(For no blood dries along the metal's edge)
As marshals peering through binoculars
Drive their offensives through my hollow mind.

O my eyes are like extravagant bees
Hugging paper gardens where words are weeds.

For at my back daily the compositors –
Aproned morticians that with lacquered sticks
Lay out the columns like coffins – hammer
Upon the bones of heretics, martyrs,
Nepmen and the conquerors finally
The clockwork victims of insolvent guns;
As I, an egret in a mere of ink,
Idly surface the black frogs thick with speech
When History having eyes but no ears
Seeks out the winged serpent in the tree.

EXCURSION TO OTTAWA

Their dufflebags sprawl like a murder
Between the seats: themselves are bored
Or boisterous. These are ignorant soldiers
Believing that when forever the violent die
The good receive their inexhaustible cow –
Grade seven and superman have arranged everything.
The other passengers are unimportant liars:
Salesmen, admen, the commercial trivia,
Blown between the lines of memoranda,
And across the aisle, disposed on thirty beds,
Two limp virgins eyes below the navel.

Slowly the train curves around rich
Suburban Westmount that squats upon a slum,
Then like a hypodermic plunges past
Uniform fenceposts into open country;
There's glazed sunlight upon the hard serrated
Fields. Air is thin slightly neurasthenic
Over the distant indiscriminate trees
That posture on hillsides gross and secretive
As women staling. Pins withdrawn suddenly
Barns collapse like real estate models. The senses
Run like swift hares along the fences.

These are the fire-lands and this a sealed train
Of cold excursionists, throats buttoned up
With yellow timetables.
                      On folded hands
The minutes drop like dandruff. The
Jetted column survives in a black foetus,
And the goats leap into their faces shrieking.

MRS. FORNHEIM, REFUGEE

Very merciful was the cancer
Which first blinding you altogether
Afterwards stopped up your hearing;
At the end when Death was nearing,
Black-gloved, to gather you in
You did not demur, or fear
One you could not see or hear.

I taught you Shakespeare's tongue, not knowing
The time and manner of your going;
Certainly if with ghosts to dwell,
German would have served as well.
Voyaging lady, I wish for you
An Englishwoman to talk to,
An unruffled listener,
And green words to say to her.

GOTHIC LANDSCAPE

They stand like penitential Augustines
These trees; and in my Jewboy mind they are monks,
Brown-robed, fearful after their long sleep in dungeons;
When I was a child one of them nearly caught me,
But I escaped, tunnelling the snow to my mother's face;
Under her grey shawl I saw God's Assyrian beard,
And a page of *lameds* racing towards me like ostriches.

I've taken no vow not to forget
The torquemadas stirring in the frosty veins:
But the cloister bells deafen me with insults,
And sallowfaced acolytes inform
The snowdrifts what to whisper against me;
Autos-da-fé make red the immaculate sky;
Come soon, O bright Tudor sun!
I do not like this monastic whiteness of winter –
It is a Christ drained of all blood.

THE BLACK HUNTSMEN

Before ever I knew men were hunting me
I knew delight as water in a glass in a pool;
The childish heart then
Was ears nose eyes twiceten fingers,
And the torpid slum street, in summer,
A cut vein of the sun
That shed goldmotes by the million
Against a boy's bare toe foot ankle knee.

Then when the old year fell out of the window
To break into snowflakes on the cold stones of City Hall
I discovered Tennyson in a secondhand bookstore;
He put his bugle for me to his bearded mouth,
And down his Aquitaine nose a diminutive King Arthur
Rode out of our grocery shop bowing to left and to right,
Bearing my mother's *sheitel* with him;
And for a whole week after that
I called my cat Launcelot.

Now I look out for the evil retinue
Making their sortie out of a forest of gold;
Afterwards their dames shall weave my *tzitzith*
Into a tapestry,
Though for myself I had preferred
A death by water or sky.

MONT ROLLAND

Pitiless towards men, I am filled with pity
For the impractical trees climbing the exhausted hillside;
Sparse, dull, with blue uneven spaces between them,
They're like the beard of an uncombed tolerant monk,
      Or a Tolstoyan disciple, circa 1890.

Below these, a straggler, a tree with such enormous boughs
It might have remembered Absalom, who dead,
Put by the aping of his father's majesty;
And one lone cedar, a sycophant, stunted,
      A buffoon with sick dreams.

While all around me, as for a favoured intruder,
There's an immense silence made for primeval birds
Or a thought to rise like a great cloud out of a crater,
A silence contained by valleys,
      Gardes Civiles in green capes.

Nevertheless the Lilliput train trivializes
The tolerant monk, the trees, and this whirlpool of silence,
Though it fling over its side like a capitalist's bequest
A memorial row
      Of blossoming cherry trees.

And the highway which seen from my window seems
A suture in the flesh of a venerable patrician,
In the distance falls like a lariat on the green necks
Of the untamed hills, that raise like wild horses
      Their dignified, astonished heads.

THE WORLD'S A TAVERN

It was a neat trick
The glass of beer floating through the air
And coming to rest on my round table –
I spit on your one good eye Polyphemus –
Then the foam fell away from the rocks
To the sound of the drinkers' voices
Like the noise from the throats
Of a thousand flushed lavatories singing together
I could see their fishhook eyes menacing me
Sly at the bottom of the cool gloom of the tavern
But I wanted to write something on the waves
Carried towards the shore on the backs of a million snails
For I knew that arrived there
They would go begging like a long poem.

To the movement then of dark and light
A Byzantine angel slid down from the smoky wall
Hovering over me with his wings outstretched –
But I saw the shape where the flat tiles were not –
Before I could make a salt out of my astonishment
There was a meadow of surf in the bay of my elbow
And while the hungry robins picked at the air
White blossoms fell on their sad faces
Held in a frame of grass and ground for sentimental poets
Who weep when they are told of such things.

I do not remember when I first noticed
The human smell below the eyes
But the ghost of an unhappy sailor
That sometimes uses my body for a night's lodging
Blew a fistful of spray into the corridor
An eye started to twinkle like a crazy lighthouse
Rocked by a giant and the waves to bob
All around me like lopped heads
Their hair as they came to the surface combed down
Like Russian peasants tolled to a green Sunday church
I think someone called me brother

And pressed my hand clammy with many misfortunes
He must have seen the smoke curling
From my ears and from my mouth too
For he or someone who resembles him closely
Suddenly began to shout fire to the lavatories.

Heaven bless the three angels who lifted me up
Though my body turned into a picnic table
With six boyhood legs on St. Helen's Island
I heard their wings brushing the foam off the rocks
But they or the boys who had drowned that summer
Made too much noise
For the robins left off picking the air
And the blossoms decomposed at my feet into a bad odour.

THE EXECUTION

Because the glowing morning
Dropped from the rooster's beak
The frozen famous statue
Was too amazed to speak

But watched my mother go and come
Like a fish in an aquarium
Sinister alone
And me upon my boycart throne.

Her cheeks were red with bargains
And she moved to the money cries
Like an enchanted dancer
With wide enchanted eyes.

The yells, the cries were frenzying;
Her cheeks grew pale with bargains:
I laid my boyhood head
Among the golden onions.

TRUMPET DAFFODIL

At last I get up and go to where
Over the back of my wooden chair
The light hangs like a wet towel.
I scan the glass for my deathless smile.

I praise the hairs on my wrist
And an indestructible egotist
Resolve this day not to glance
At what I may not influence.

Then I thresh out whether the literati
With faces like garlic when I die
Will lay their opera hats on my coffin
And their voices soften.

To the devil with meditation
Which leads to nowhere and on;
I'd rather take a basket
Of opera hats to someone else's casket.

I look out of the window
At the people hurrying below;
These carry their disenchantment graveward
Like an identity card.

I think the sun
Has already begun
To burn their futility and need
And themselves to a brown weed.

TO A VERY OLD WOMAN

Old woman, your face is a halo of praise
That excludes nothing, not even Death;
    I have looked upon your waxy and virginal torso
    And I see you now as a frail candle
Whose flame, the initial sputter of ignition over,
Burns gently and with composure.

So the first taste of death was bitter.
Now you burn with a composed glow
    Listening, half-amused like a superior person,
    To your bridegroom which is the Darkness
While each hour of your lovely embrace
Descends in ecstatic beads of silence.

Old woman,
What does he say, your bridegroom?

That his child, Death, grows in my womb.

What else, old woman?

That only my white and virginal skin
Seals off the darkness from the death within.

Old woman, with face ageless like snow,
What will you do now?

Flame serenely
Till like a warmed candle
I curve over
The arm of my hurrying bridegroom and lover.

Is that all, old woman?

Yes...
No. When Death and Darkness embrace
Over me
I shall have no face
I shall be utterly gone.
Use the blackened wick
For a headstone.

LOVE THE CONQUEROR WORM

Mid-August the frenzied cicadas
Apprise the scene-shifters
Where each prop goes:
  Where the dark empery of bush,
And where the spacious blossomers.

Now lofty for the spinning year,
For the stripling I see pass
Dragging the summer by the ear;
  The flooding sun,
And the green fires in the grass

I pardon Nature her insanities,
The perversity in flesh and fern;
I forget her lecheries,
  Her paragram:
Love The Conqueror Worm

And praise these oaks which bare,
Straining, the hoar
Frost on them, stand each winter there
  Like courtly masochists
Whimpering "Encore! Encore!"

VEXATA QUAESTIO

I fixing my eyes upon a tree
Maccabean among the dwarfed
    Stalks of summer
Listened for ship's sound and birdsong
And felt the bites of insects
    Expiring in my arms' hairs.

And there among the green prayerful birds
Among the corn I heard
    The chaffering blades:
"You are no flydung on cherry blossoms,
Among two-legged lice
    You have the gift of praise.

Give your stripped body to the sun
Your sex to any skilled
    And pretty damsel;
From the bonfire
Of your guilts make
    A blazing Greek sun."

Then the wind which all day
Had run regattas through the fields
    Grew chill, became
A tree-dismantling wind;

The sun went down
    And called my brown skin in.

CEMETERY IN AUGUST

In August, white butterflies
Engage twig and rock;
Love-sheaths bloom in convenient fissures
On a desiccated stalk;
The generation of Time brings
Rind, shell, delicate wings

And mourners. Amidst this
Summer's babble of small noises
They weep, or interject
Their resentful human voices;
At timely intervals
I am aware of funerals.

And these iambic stones
Honouring who-knows-what bones
Seem in the amber sunlight
Patient and confounded,
Like men enduring an epoch
Or one bemused by proofs of God.

DEATH OF MOISHE LAZAROVITCH

My father's coffin pointed me to this:
O arrogant with new life his black beard
Fierce and stiff and partner to the dark wood
Sent me the way to what I most had feared

Became at the last a ring of bright light,
A well whose wall of mourning faces turned
My sighs to silence to a deep wound
Which stained the outstretched figure as it burned.

I swear it burned! If not, why the bright light
Like a tall post that had caught the sun's ray?
White the figure was and bright O so bright,
I have not seen its equal since that day.

I do not know how they lifted him up
Or held the vessel near their mourning silk,
But their going was like a roar of flames
And Matter sang in my ears like poured milk.

TO THE GIRLS OF MY GRADUATING CLASS

Wanting for their young limbs praise,
Their thighs, hips, and saintly breasts,
They grow from awkwardness to delight,
Their mouths made perfect with the air
About them and the sweet rage in the blood,
The delicate trouble in their veins.

Intolerant as happiness, suddenly
They'll dart like bewildered birds;
For there's no mercy in that bugler Time
That excites against their virginity
The massed infantry of days, nor in the tendrils
Greening on their enchanted battlements.

Golda, Fruma, Dinnie, Elinor,
My saintly wantons, passionate nuns;
O light-footed daughters, your unopened
Brittle beauty troubles an aging man
Who hobbles after you a little way
Fierce and ridiculous.

IN THE MIDST OF MY FEVER

In the midst of my fever, large
as Europe's pain,
The birds hopping on the blackened wires
were instantly electrocuted;
Bullfrogs were slaughtered in large numbers
to the sound of their own innocent thrummings;
The beautiful whores of the king
found lovers and disappeared;
The metaphysician sniffed the thought before him
like a wrinkled fruit;
And the envoys meeting on the sunny quay
for once said the truth about the weather.
In the midst of this rich confusion, a
miracle happened: someone
quietly performed a good deed;
And the grey imperial lions, growling, carried
the news in their jaws.
I heard them. So did Androcles.

19

O from the height of my fever, the sweat
    ran down my hairless limbs
Like the blood from the condemned patron
    of specially unlucky slaves. Then, O then
Great Caesar's legions halted before my troubled ear,
    Jacobean in Time's double exposure.
My brassy limbs stiffened
    like a trumpet blast; surely
The minutes now covered with gold-dust
    will in time
Drop birdlime upon the handsomest
    standard-bearer,
Caesar himself discover the exhaustible flesh,
    my lips
White with prophecy aver before him.
But the conqueror's lips are like pearls,
    and he hurls his javelin at the target sky.

In the depth of my gay fever, I saw my limbs
    like Hebrew letters
Twisted with too much learning. I was
Seer, sensualist, or fake ambassador; the tyrant
    who never lied
And cried like an infant after he'd had to
    to succour his people.
Then I disengaging my arm to bless,
In an eyeblink became the benediction
    dropped from the Roman's fingers;
Nudes, nodes, nodules, became all one,
    existence seamless and I
Crawling solitary upon the globe of marble
    waited for the footfall which never came.
And I thought of Time's wretches and of some
    dear ones not yet dead
And of Coleridge taking laudanum.

SEVEN O'CLOCK LECTURE

Filling their ears
With the immortal claptrap of poetry,
These singular lies with the power
    to get themselves believed,
The permanent bloom on all time-infected things;
Indicating the will to falsehood in the hearts of men,
The music in a pismire's walk, the necessary glory of dung,
    immortal coal of the universe,
Leibniz's mirroring monads, daybeams of consciousness

I see their heads sway at the seven o'clock lecture;
I imagine they forget the hungers, the desperate fears
    in the hollow parts of their bodies,
The physiological smells, the sardine cans, the flitch of bacon,
The chicken bones gathered neatly
        to one side of the plate;
Life is horrifying, said Cézanne,
             but this is not
    what he meant who picked flowers blooming
    in the slaughterhouse; he meant the slit throats,
The bear traps smeared with blood, the iron goads,
  the frightened
    servant-girl's Caesarian,
And this planet dancing about Apollo,
    the blood drying and shining in the sun,
Turning to Titians, beauty, the Arts . . .

My heart is parted like the Red Sea.
It cracks!
And where the cleft is formed
The BARBARI carrying their chromium gods
    on their sunburnt arms and shoulders
Ride on my nightmares, a hot desert wind
    pushing them swiftly toward these faces
    washed clean of Death and Agony;

God! God! Shall I jiggle my gored haunches
      to make these faces laugh?
Shall the blood rain down on these paper masks?
Flammonde, Light of the World, in this well-lit
      fluorescent age you are a failure, lacking savvy;
Gregor Metamorphosis, fantastic bogeylouse,
      you are without meaning to those who nightly
      bed down on well-aired sheets;
In the fifth row someone pulls out a laundered emotion
      and wipes his long, false nose.

At last the bell goes, Lear lamenting Cordelia, the wall's
      piercing cry . . .

        You may grieve now, gentlemen.

COMPOSITION IN LATE SPRING

When Love ensnares my mind unbidden
      I am lost in the usual way
On a crowded street or avenue
Where I am lord of all the marquees,
And the traffic cop moving his lips
      Like a poet composing
Whistles a discovery of sparrows
About my head.

My mind full of goats and pirates
      And simpler than a boy's,
I walk through a forest of white arms
That embrace me like window-shoppers;
Friends praise me like a Turkish delight
      Or a new kind of suspender
And children love me
Like a story.

Conscience more flat than cardboard
        Over the gap in a sole,
I avoid the fanatic whose subway
Collapsed in his brain;
There's a sinking, but the madonna
        Who clings to my hairlock
Is saved: on shore the damned ones
Applaud with the vigour of bees.

The sparrows' golden plummeting
        From fearful rooftop
Shows the flesh dying into sunshine.
Fled to the green suburbs, Death
Lies scared to death under a heap of bones.
        Beauty buds from mire
And I, a singer in season, observe
Death is a name for beauty not in use.

No one is more happy, none can do more tricks.
        The sun melts like butter
Over my sweetcorn thoughts;
And, at last, both famous and good
I'm a Doge, a dog
        At the end of a terrace
Where poems like angels like flakes of powder
Quaver above my prickling skin.

THE BIRTH OF TRAGEDY

And me happiest when I compose poems.
 Love, power, the huzza of battle
 are something, are much;
yet a poem includes them like a pool
 water and reflection.
In me, nature's divided things –
 tree, mould on tree –
 have their fruition;
I am their core. Let them swap,
bandy, like a flame swerve
I am their mouth; as a mouth I serve.

And I observe how the sensual moths
 big with odour and sunshine
 dart into the perilous shrubbery;
or drop their visiting shadows
 upon the garden I one year made
of flowering stone to be a footstool
 for the perfect gods:
 who, friends to the ascending orders,
sustain all passionate meditations
and call down pardons
for the insurgent blood.

A quiet madman, never far from tears,
 I lie like a slain thing
 under the green air the trees
inhabit, or rest upon a chair
 towards which the inflammable air
tumbles on many robins' wings;
 noting how seasonally
 leaf and blossom uncurl
and living things arrange their death,
while someone from afar off
blows birthday candles for the world.

MAXIE

Son, braggart, and thrasher,
is the cock's querulous strut
in air, an aggression.

At sight of him as at the sound
of "raw" my mind half-creates
tableaus, seas, immensities.

Mornings, I've seen his good looks
drop into the spider's mitre
pinned up between stem and stem.

All summer the months grovel
and bound at his heels like spaniels.
All seasons are occult toys to him,

a thing he takes out of the cupboard
certain there are no more
than two, at the most four.

I suppose, spouse, what I wanted
was to hold the enduring folds
of your dress. Now there's this.

This energetic skin-and-bones. You'll see,
he'll pummel the two of us to death,
laughing at our wrinkled amazement.

Yes, though his upthrust into air
is more certain
than delight or unreason,

and his active pellmell feet
scatter promises, elations
of breast and womb;

yet his growing up so neighbourly
to grass, us, and qualifying cobwebs
has given me a turn for sculptured stone.

METZINGER: GIRL WITH A BIRD

Your eyes, heavy-lidded,
half-closed, make of sadness
itself a caprice, or seem to.
I have the feeling, miss,
you dream too much
of flight – on winter evenings!
Yet the mist
of those nerveless evenings
lives in your clouded eyes.

Your face
tilts toward the gay edifice
through whose casements
birds might go in and out;
and your elbow is,
to be sure,
a gesture that makes known
your will – yet hardly more;
the flexures of your breast and skirt
turn like an appetite also there.

Too small
for a swan, a raping Zeus:
the still bird, symbol
of decession and freedom,
that you fold between your full
breasts
pins you by a paradox
against the air.
There is no happiness here;

Only the desire
of the impotent, the weak
who, if they wish to speak,
must first grow indignant;
It taxes my brain,
miss, to guess at the monster
or tyrant

who inhabits the shuttered building
the lines of your head and breasts
turn away from with such disdain.

NEW TABLES

I do not want power
And great wealth I never cared for;
Most people, when I see them running after these things,
Fill me with anxiety and compassion;
I am anxious about them
And about myself who must unavoidably deal with them
These sick people whom no one loves or understands,
Whom even the gods
      with their lovely waterfalls and mists
Have completely expunged from their memory

These ailing people are each other's death
Sooner or later they fall upon each other's swords
They die into each other without valour or pity
Or fold noiselessly into each other like grey shadows;
They expire quietly like poisonous mushrooms
On a forest floor
And are shrivelled up by the sun
Into a fine white powder waiting to make greater sense
In some other, more fortunate duration

For myself I like nothing better
Than to go walking down the unpaved streets
With the sun for my constant companion;
I like the way the dogs greet the two of us
With plenty of tail-waggings, rushes, innocent barkings.
When the children lift their faces
Like delicate flowers to be touched lightly
I feel an emotion no saint, no, nor mystic
Ever felt before me at this arrangement of sudden glory;

Perhaps the humble grasses in the fields
Understand this whitest ecstasy,
And the bare trees in late April
Waiting patiently for their gift of leaves

At such moments, poor and powerless,
I am so full of blessing I think I could babble
The meaningless religious words, the formulas of contrition,
The bewildered ghost-sounds, ghost-meanings of old men;
And if I do not it's because I wish to startle the earth
Bored to death by the prodigal centuries,
Their white ashes combed by fierce winds
Like the streaming hairs of frenzied anchorites,
The yea-sayers of hammered conviction;
And because thereby, decked out in green and gold,
She gains a greater glory –
The finer triumph – to force this praise from me,
An atheist, shivering with blessed ecstasy

PROLOGUE TO THE LONG PEA-SHOOTER

A friend tells me I must not write
About the toilers and their sad plight,
That poetry like dress admits of fashion
And this is not the year for passion.
He thinks the times will change: tomorrow
The critic may approve of sorrow,
And anger be no blemish in a verse
Which today must neither taunt nor curse.
For now lampooners, themselves grown sick,
Prefer poets with a touch of colic
Who'll speak in soft, deflated tones
That menace no one's sleep or bones.
One may, he concedes, clear his throat
To flute a meek religious note

For it's the season now to cavil
At Original Sin and Evil,
And for the dull-eyed philistine
To be mistook for an Olympian
Since none in this country can tell
The one from the other very well.

For since our neighbours get their creed
From the latest comic strip they read
(Though kind, they're dumb – they come no dumber!)
You can spoof them winter, spring, and summer.
Let them but see a tale in print
They think at once the truth lies in't
And hotly with one voice they'll swear
They see hippogriffs coupling in the air;
That elephants fly, that gramophones swim –
There is no fable too gross for them!
The press on a rampage, hear them cry
With virtuous anger: "The knaves must die!"
The press grown quiet – why, the sods
Let their wrath expire, and virtue nods.

Consider therefore to what end you write
And whether vanity can survive this sight:
Your tomes piled ingloriously in a heap,
Your craft and wisdom sold absurdly cheap;
Assonance, sprung rhythm, internal rhyme,
The whole glittering shebang not worth a dime;
For of fourteen million odd citizens
No more than five have taste or sense
And these, alas, though not fools
Belong to different sects and schools
Fanatic in belief some rival
Mode of metaphor lacks wit and style;
Or fine poets themselves, they prefer
To see your thin volume gather
A coating of oblivious dust
Lest a sold edition and success rust

That friendship which the fates erect
Upon equal misfortune and neglect.

Resolve before ink you try
That your books may not remaindered lie;
Think only of kudos and a name
And failing greatness, acquire fame:
Assiduously learn the art to please
The pimps in the academies –
Their friendly syrop on the radio
May help to sell a book or so;
(I mean to give them no offence,
For these are pimps with a difference,
And allow this as their best excuse –
They pimp, it's true, but for some muse!)
Yes, be wise, plagiarize: above all,
Avoid ambiguous words like 'ball'
Or 'ass' or even harmless 'cans':
They give offence to puritans,
And robust males to whom a virgin
Is dearer far than any sturgeon.
And say nothing long, say nothing loud
To charm and please that motley crowd
Of·cultured hags who like a poem
To waft them far from spouse and home
Or bring a fine synthetic gloom
Into their modernized living-room;
Refinement be your aim to melt the sort
Who take their verse as they take their port
Entirely by label and repute
And with no more sense than a new-born newt
Seek out the poet that is most sought:
If it's Eliot – it's Eliot they've got!
But if you have the gifts of Reaney
You may help your verse by being zany,
Or write as bleakly in a pinch
As Livesay, Smith, and Robert Finch;
And be admired for a brand-new pot
If you're as empty as Marriott;

I'll say nothing about Dudek:
The rhyme's too easy – speck or wreck;
And be not right and be not left,
But mediocre like the C.C.F.

But the soundest, most successful plan
Is to compose like Douglas Le Pan:
Appear, though men and nations reeled,
A Lampman on a battlefield;
Express in words vacuous and quaint
The cultured Englishman's complaint
That decency is never sovereign,
That reason ought to, but doesn't govern –
That maids have holes, and men must find them
(Alas, that Nature WILL so blind them!)
In short, here's the sum of this advice:
Say nothing, but modulate the voice;
What though the lines lack heart and brain,
One can wrap the mess in cellophane;
The trick's to make quick and often
Neat chromium handles for a coffin
For critics with the nose of a setter
For verse that's dead – the deader the better!
These buzzards have no praise for him
Who cannot learn to tack and trim,
The honest bard who'll out and say
By how much profit exceeds the pay;
Or one who because his heart is pure
Will not affect to use 'manure'
Instead of that four-letter word
That is less often seen than heard,
But paints the world with sober brush
Though reviewers and Mazola Roche
Who type on their cash register
Declare such writing sinister.

Well, I tell my friend that I've written
About the parts where I've been bitten;
I write about where the shoe pinches;
I also write about the wenches;

Their lips, their hips, and other beauty
(Laying them is a man's first duty!)
Of all sad things the saddest sight
Are pubic hairs turned grey and white,
Or thinned by age, a spiritless down,
Ranged like a battered rusty crown
Or a harbour broken at the centre
Where no boat shall leave or enter.
Though of late, since I'm growing old,
And no longer wear my pants' fly rolled
I like to engage over a glass
Retired clergymen put out to grass;
Their craws well-stuffed with fish and fowl
They discourse sweetly upon the soul,
For I've noted often how the sight
Of a ravished duck will speed the flight
Of men's thoughts towards the ineffable,
The inane, and the indecipherable
Though it's difficult such times to tell
If they're moved to glory by taste or smell,
And whether it's their souls that yearn
Or what is speaking is some heartburn.
Strange that human blood can spiritualize
The breast of chicken or its thighs
And turn by wondrous transmutation
The creature's flesh into aspiration;
Strange, that pig en route towards the anus
Can disintegrate into loud hosannas!

So with such wit as I can muster
I surmise I've brought a lustre
To our national verse which before
Was lacking spirit and a bore,
Genteel, dull, and quite anæmic
To please a Bowell or Jasper Shittick;
And though the fat excitable fleas
Who breed well in our universities
Aver my stuff is unreadable,
Unedifying and unbeautiful

What fool will pay much or close
Attention to these same castratos,
What race will read what they have said
Who have my poems to read instead?

MISUNDERSTANDING

I placed
my hand
upon
her thigh.

By the way
she moved
away
I could see
her devotion
to literature
was not
perfect.

RAIN AT LA MINERVE

All day the heavens have opened up
and it has rained rained rained
rained
with the maliciousness of a minor poet.

It's not my element; I cannot live with it.
Perhaps because my forbears were thrifty merchants
it dispirits me to know
so much excellent water
        is going to waste, is going under bridges
to serve an outworn metaphor, expending
so much effort to so little effect.

Snow I can take, if I have to:
if only because of the satisfaction I have
in supposing that snow
is what someone has done to rain,
his contempt for it published in a million white bulletins.

It has rained for three days and three nights
and the vegetation is lush and very green.
They say Ireland is like that, the green rolling hillsides
a brogue in your eye and a lilt in both ears.
But I have never wanted to go to Ireland
now that her great sons are dead
(real Irish giants – Shaw and Joyce and Yeats
– not mythical ones)
and each little green blade, a rosary around it,
saying a paternoster to the wind.

Ireland? More like Africa.
I'm afraid to peer under my armpits, I might find
        tropical ferns growing sideways; and my limbs
      have begun to feel thick and rubberish and tubular.
I have the feeling if I step on the floor
                of my room,
water will splash out of my ankles
as from an old boot or water bag.
The rain makes numerous thunders in my head,
      but it could be the tom-toms
        announcing the white man's love for the blacks.

Help me, someone.

I imagine my body is the whole steaming
                continent of Africa,
and millions of animals are squishing
through the torrential jungle rains inside me
but one lion in particular
        I see him, the fierce proud beast –
roars, and roars again:
roars roars roars roars

LOOK, THE LAMBS
ARE ALL AROUND US!

Your figure, love,
curves itself
into a man's memory;
or to put it the way
a junior prof
at Mount Allison might,
Helen with her thick
absconding limbs
about the waist
of Paris
did no better.

Hell, my back's sunburnt
from so much love-making
in the open air.
The Primate (somebody
made a monkey of him)
and the Sanhedrin
(long on the beard, short
on the brain)
send envoys to say
they don't approve.
You never see them, love.
You toss me in the air
with such abandon,
they take to their heels and run.
I tell you
each kiss of yours
is like a blow on the head!

What luck, what luck to be loved
by the one girl
in this Presbyterian
country
who knows how to give
a man pleasure.

ON FIRST LOOKING INTO
STALIN'S COFFIN

When I was
a burning idealist
I wanted very much
for Comrade Joe
to live forever

he was so good
for the unborn children
and for the grave cows
that gave
extra yields of milk
whenever he riffled
their tails
with a *pieteletka*

Jubilating
like a bleeding
bride
I even wrote a poem
which began
"Comrade Trotsky
is dead . . ."
after one of the boys
had polished him off
with an icepick

That shattering minute
was it remorse
went suddenly
like steel
to the Vohzd's head
Or was he
brainstruck
thinking how feasible
to recreate with him
and Comrade Death
an old triumvirate

Kaput
in his coffin
lies the world's
benefactor
giving off odours
but no answers

THE COLD GREEN ELEMENT

At the end of the garden walk
the wind and its satellite wait for me;
their meaning I will not know
             until I go there,
but the black-hatted undertaker

who, passing, saw my heart beating in the grass,
is also going there. Hi, I tell him,
a great squall in the Pacific blew a dead poet
             out of the water,
who now hangs from the city's gates.

Crowds depart daily to see it, and return
with grimaces and incomprehension;
if its limbs twitched in the air
             they would sit at its feet
peeling their oranges.

And turning over I embrace like a lover
the trunk of a tree, one of those
for whom the lightning was too much
             and grew a brilliant
hunchback with a crown of leaves.

The ailments escaped from the labels
of medicine bottles are all fled to the wind;
I've seen myself lately in the eyes
             of old women,
spent streams mourning my manhood,

in whose old pupils the sun became
a bloodsmear on broad catalpa leaves
and hanging from ancient twigs,
        my murdered selves
sparked the air like the muted collisions

of fruit. A black dog howls down my blood,
a black dog with yellow eyes;
he too by someone's inadvertence
        saw the bloodsmear
on the broad catalpa leaves.

But the furies clear a path for me to the worm
who sang for an hour in the throat of a robin,
and misled by the cries of young boys
        I am again
a breathless swimmer in that cold green element.

THE IMPROVED BINOCULARS

Below me the city was in flames:
the firemen were the first to save
themselves. I saw steeples fall on their knees.

I saw an agent kick the charred bodies
from an orphanage to one side, marking
the site carefully for a future speculation.

Lovers stopped short of the final spasm
and went off angrily in opposite directions,
their elbows held by giant escorts of fire.

Then the dignitaries rode across the bridges
under an auricle of light which delighted them,
noting for later punishment those that went before.

And the rest of the populace, their mouths
distorted by an unusual gladness, bawled thanks
to this comely and ravaging ally, asking

Only for more light with which to see
their neighbour's destruction.

All this I saw through my improved binoculars.

I WOULD
FOR YOUR SAKE BE GENTLE

I would for your sake be gentle
Be, believe me, other than I am:
What, what madness is it that hurls me
Sundays against your Sunday calm?

True, there's enough gall in my ducts
To cover an area, and more:
But why you – free from evil, poor bird?
Why you – my heart and saviour?

I swear I'm damned to so hate and rage.
But your fair innocence is my guilt;
And the stream that you make clear
I must, to fog my image, fill with silt.

Bear with me, bear with me –
Your goodness, gift so little understood
Even by the angels I suppose
And by us here somewhat undervalued

Is what I hold to when madness comes.
It is the soft night against which I flare
Rocketwise, and when I fall
See my way back by my own embers.

ENEMIES

The young carpenter
        who works on his house
has no definition for me.

I am for him
        a book. A face in a book.
Finally a face.

The sunlight
        on the white paper
The sunlight on the easy

Summer chair
        is the same sunlight
which glints rosily

From his hammer.
        He is aware suddenly
of connections: I

Am embroiled
        in the echoing sound
of his implement

As it slides nails
        into the resistant wood
from which later, later

Coffins will emerge
        as if by some monstrous
parturition. Is it any wonder

He so mislikes me
        seeing his handiwork
robed in black?

Seeing I shatter
      his artifact of space
with that which is

Forever dislodging
      the framework for
its own apprehension?

Over the wall
      of sound I see
his brutal grin of victory

Made incomplete
      by the white sunlit
paper I hold on my knee.

He has no metal
      gauge to take in
a man with a book

And yet his
      awkward shadow
falls on each page.

We are implicated,
      in each other's presence
by the sun, the third party

(Itself unimplicated)
      and only for a moment
reconciled to each other's

Necessary existence
      by the sight
of our neighbour's

Excited boy
      whom some God, I conjecture,
bounces for His joy.

41

SONG FOR NAOMI

Who is that in the tall grasses singing
By herself, near the water?
I can not see her
But can it be her
Than whom the grasses so tall
Are taller,
My daughter,
My lovely daughter?

Who is that in the tall grasses running
Beside her, near the water?
She can not see there
Time that pursued her
In the deep grasses so fast
And faster
And caught her,
My foolish daughter.

What is the wind in the fair grass saying
Like a verse, near the water?
Saviours that over
All things have power
Make Time himself grow kind
And kinder
That sought her,
My little daughter.

Who is that at the close of the summer
Near the deep lake? Who wrought her
Comely and slender?
Time but attends and befriends her
Than whom the grasses though tall
Are not taller,
My daughter,
My gentle daughter.

METAMORPHOSIS

I looked up expecting fire
        To find instead
Red flowers and inert stalks
And through the grasses
Snapped from too much heat
Irregular shadows in the trees
        Of leaf on leaf.

New butterflies went round my chair
        And stitched me there;
I could not move but sat as one
Hypnotized by the sun;
Then as my limbs grew mould,
Grew stems and grass
        I saw a thrush.

And with that attention
        Envy lends
I steered its sunward flight
Till, dispossessed, I caught
The motion of the bird
And heard within my blood
        Its singing pleasure.

FOR MY DETRACTORS

You are astonished
when I open my mouth
to speak of poetry

Who is this butcher, you ask,
with his nose
broken and twisted
like a boxer's?

Look, you exclaim,
at the mat of hair
that covers his neck
and his heavy gait
like that of a startled bruin's

The curious among you
and the more impudent
approach quietly
to scrutinize my ears

By the slow looks
you throw one another
I see you conclude
degeneracy or worse

Ah, my detractors,
this is a rough profession
I have chosen

I need all my strength

And if my face scares,
so much the better;
I have that more space
for myself, and for quiet,
and for the poems
that I gather
with a tenderness
you could never
imagine or intuit.

LETTER FROM A STRAW MAN

I loved you, Bobbo, even when you knuckled me
And pulled the straw out of my breast,
Pretending to weep yet secretly glad to note
How yellow and summer-dry the stuff was.

You will surely recall how amazed
We both were the straw was endless;
At the time I did not know it was your fingers
Made the straw grow there and blaze

Yellow in the fierce sunlight. . . . How when
I once caught your cold blue eye
It first burned like sulphur, but affected
Let down a tear like a drop of dirty sea-water

Into my prized open chest; though after
That encounter of our eyes, your own –
The pitiful one – grew into a porcelain saucer
White and blind. That I could understand.

But why did you give great handfuls
To the visiting firemen? And when the mayor
Asked for some to decorate his fireplace,
Why did you not refuse? No, rather,

Plunging your green delicate fingers
Into my gaping breast you drew
Out for him the longest stalk
Which he snatched with a cough and a compelling eye.

I have left you for another,
Who wears black panties and is as crazy as the birds;
But when the straw comes away in her hands
She is careful to burn it immediately afterwards.

THE BULL CALF

The thing could barely stand. Yet taken
from his mother and the barn smells
he still impressed with his pride,
with the promise of sovereignty in the way
his head moved to take us in.
The fierce sunlight tugging the maize from the ground
licked at his shapely flanks.
He was too young for all that pride.
I thought of the deposed Richard II.

"No money in bull calves," Freeman had said.
The visiting clergyman rubbed the nostrils
now snuffing pathetically at the windless day.
"A pity," he sighed.
My gaze slipped off his hat toward the empty sky
that circled over the black knot of men,
over us and the calf waiting for the first blow.

Struck,
the bull calf drew in his thin forelegs
as if gathering strength for a mad rush . . .
tottered . . . raised his darkening eyes to us,
and I saw we were at the far end
of his frightened look, growing smaller and smaller
till we were only the ponderous mallet
that flicked his bleeding ear
and pushed him over on his side, stiffly,
like a block of wood.

Below the hill's crest
the river snuffled on the improvised beach.
We dug a deep pit and threw the dead calf into it.
It made a wet sound, a sepulchral gurgle,
as the warm sides bulged and flattened.
Settled, the bull calf lay as if asleep,
one foreleg over the other,
bereft of pride and so beautiful now,
without movement, perfectly still in the cool pit.
I turned away and wept.

THE FERTILE MUCK

There are brightest apples on those trees
    but until I, fabulist, have spoken
they do not know their significance
or what other legends are hung like garlands
    on their black boughs twisting
like a rumour. The wind's noise is empty.

Nor are the winged insects better off
    though they wear my crafty eyes
wherever they alight. Stay here, my love;
you will see how delicately they deposit
    me on the leaves of elms
or fold me in the orient dust of summer.

And if in August joiners and bricklayers
    are thick as flies around us
building expensive bungalows for those
who do not need them, unless they release
    me roaring from their moth-proofed cupboards
their buyers will have no joy, no ease.

I could extend their rooms for them without cost
    and give them crazy sundials
to tell the time with, but I have noticed
how my irregular footprint horrifies them
    evenings and Sunday afternoons:
they spray for hours to erase its shadow.

How to dominate reality? Love is one way;
    imagination another. Sit here
beside me, sweet; take my hard hand in yours.
We'll mark the butterflies disappearing over the hedge
    with tiny wristwatches on their wings:
our fingers touching the earth, like two Buddhas.

CHOKECHERRIES

The sun's gift –

but the leaves a sickly green;
the more exposed curling, showing
a bleached white, many with ragged
holes;
Caterpillars have been
here
sliding their slow destructive bodies
over them.

I think of them, the leaves, as hoplites
or as anything ingloriously
useful,
suffering, dying . . .

But the chokecherries,
ah;
Still, the leaves' sacrifice
is acrid on the tongue.

SACRAMENT BY THE WATER

How shall I sing the accomplished waters
Whose teeming cells make green my hopes
How shall the Sun at daybreak marry us
Twirling these waters like a hoop.

Gift of the waters that sing
Their eternal passion for the sky,
Your cunning beauty in a wave of tumult
Drops an Eden about your thighs.

Green is the singing singing water
And green is every joyous leaf
White myrtle's in your hand and in the other
The hairy apple bringing life.

RED CHOKECHERRIES

In the sun
The chokecherries are a deep red.
They are like clusters of red jewels.

They are like small rubies
For a young queen who is small and graceful.
When the leaves turn, I see her white shoulder.

They are too regal to eat
And reduce to moist yellow pits.
I will let the air masticate them

And the bold maggot-making sun.
So I shall hardly notice
How perfection of form is overthrown.

SONG FOR A LATE HOUR

No one told me
to beware your bracelets,
the winds I could expect
from your small breasts.
No one told me
the tumult of your hair.
When a lock touched me
I knew the sensations
of shattering glass.

Your kissings put
blue waters around me.
I would look at you
with bold Cretan mirth:
I would forget
I am a cringing semite,
a spaniel suffering
about your tight skirts.

I slabber for your rippling
hips, your white shoulders.
I am sick
with love of you. Girl, o girl,
let our washed limbs make
a perverse Star of David
and cones of flesh,
Cythera all night
at my silvered back.

THE WAY OF THE WORLD

It has taken me long, Lygdamus,
    to learn that humans, barring
a few saints, are degenerate
    or senseless.
The senseless ones are never by design
    evil; but get in your way
like the ugly stumps of trees; order
    bad taste or out of boredom
start long wars
        where one's counted on
to dredge up manliness, fortitude, and valour
    for their stupefactions.

But wicked are the clever ones.
    Cultured and adept
they will seduce a friend's dear one
with praises of her husband on their lips.

As for the wife
    a little alcohol parts her thighs.
Do not blame her: her husband's name
on the seducer's lips
    makes her the eagerer to satisfy,
teaches her she lies with her very spouse.
And that way is best: no pricks of inwit,
    but the novelty's stab of pleasure is there.

Therefore give me only lovers.
    Come, my latest one, sloe-eyed,
your firm breasts whirling like astonished globes
    before my eyes cross-eyed with lust;
though my legs are bandy
        the heart's stout
and this provocative member smooth and unwrinkled.
Till the morning parts us, I'll lie beside you
    your nipple at my tired mouth
and one hand of mine
        on your black curling fleece.

ON SEEING THE STATUETTES
OF EZEKIEL AND JEREMIAH
IN THE CHURCH OF NOTRE-DAME

They have given you French names
    and made you captive, my rugged
troublesome compatriots;
    your splendid beards, here, are epicene,
plaster white
        and your angers
unclothed with Palestinian hills quite lost
in this immense and ugly edifice.

You are bored – I see it – sultry prophets
    with priests and nuns
(What coarse jokes must pass between you!)
    and with those morbidly religious
i.e. my prize brother-in-law
            ex-Lawrencian
pawing his rosary, and his wife
sick with many guilts.

Believe me I would gladly take you
    from this spidery church
its bad melodrama, its musty smell of candle
    and set you both free again
in no make-believe world
        of sin and penitence
but the sunlit square opposite
alive at noon with arrogant men.

Yet cheer up Ezekiel and you Jeremiah
    who were once cast into a pit;
I shall not leave you here incensed, uneasy
    among alien Catholic saints
but shall bring you from time to time
        my hot Hebrew heart
as passionate as your own, and stand
with you here awhile in aching confraternity.

FROM COLONY TO NATION

A dull people,
but the rivers of this country
are wide and beautiful

A dull people
enamoured of childish games,
but food is easily come by
and plentiful

Some with a priest's voice
in their cage of ribs: but
on high mountain-tops and in thunderstorms
the chirping is not heard

Deferring to beadle and censor;
not ashamed for this,
but given over to horseplay,
the making of money

A dull people, without charm
or ideas,
settling into the clean empty look
of a Mountie or dairy farmer
as into a legacy

One can ignore them
(the silences, the vast distances help)
and suppose them at the bottom
of one of the meaner lakes,
their bones not even picked for souvenirs.

ON BEING BITTEN BY A DOG

A doctor for mere lucre
performed an unnecessary operation
making my nose nearly
as crooked as himself

Another for a similar reason
almost blinded me

A poet famous
for his lyrics of love
and renunciation
toils at the seduction of my wife

And the humans who would like to kill me
are legion

Only once have I been bitten by a dog.

NAUSICÄA

"I'm the sort of girl
    you must first tell you love."
"I love you," I said.
She gave herself to me then
    and I enjoyed her on her perfumed bed.

By the gods, the pleasure in her small
    wriggling body was so great,
  I had spoken no lecherous falsehood.
Now not I nor my beloved,
    such is our heat,
can wait for either words or scented sheet
but on her or my raincoat go roughly to it.

BARGAIN

In fourteen years
    of married bliss
not once have I been disloyal
to my wife;
and you, I am told, are still
a virgin.

If you are set
    to barter your maidenhead
for my unheard-of fidelity,
call me between three and five tomorrow
and it is done.

BY ECSTASIES PERPLEXED

By that, by this, by sharp ecstasies perplexed,
illumined, a saint streaked with foibles,
    I wore at the heart a hairshirt of fire,
wrapped my thighs in a loincloth of bees.

Honour foreswore and talent, and with these
burnished those bluedyed baubles which hang
    amorously from sad and arid bantam trees
in one-room apartments cheaply furnished.

Yet now with lust and indignation spent
and even remorse and other troubles
    I ask whether by deliberate will I went
or frenzy at a woman's beauty.

And cannot answer. But recall
a flaxen-haired boy five years old
    who one bad night put fire to his gown
and watched the flames about him rise blue and gold.

WOMAN

Vain and not to trust
unstable as wind,
as the wind ignorant;
shallow, her laugh
jarring my mended teeth.
I spit out
the loose silver
from my aching mouth.

With candid gaze
she meets my jealous
look, and is false.
Yet I am lost, lost.
Beauty and pleasure,
fatal gifts,
she brings in her thighs,
in her small amorous body.

O not remembering
her derision of me,
I plunge like a corkscrew
into her softness,
her small wicked body
and there, beyond reproach,
I roar like a sick lion
between her breasts.

RAIN

The wind blew hard in the trees
And palegreen was the wet grass;
I love you, Love, my Sweet said
And gave her false mouth to kiss.

Huge leopard spots the rain put
On the stone near where we sat;
An obscure song at our feet
Sang the troubled rivulet.

In front the black road went by,
A panther in search of prey;
Between some mouldering firs
I lay down her bleeding corse.

The wind blew hard in the trees
And screeched in the low briars;
I loved you truly, I said
And kissed her false dead mouth.

The rain fell, decaying eyes
And small ears: how green the moss!
Let her red lips kiss the rot
In their last quiver of death.

The white rain shall knit her shroud
And clean my hands of her blood;
The cottage on the round lake
Blind that eye like a cataract.

WHATEVER ELSE
POETRY IS FREEDOM

Whatever else poetry is freedom.
Forget the rhetoric, the trick of lying
All poets pick up sooner or later. From the river,
Rising like the thin voice of grey castratos – the mist;
Poplars and pines grow straight but oaks are gnarled;
Old codgers must speak of death, boys break windows;
Women lie honestly by their men at last.

And I who gave my Kate a blackened eye
Did to its vivid changing colours
Make up an incredible musical scale;
And now I balance on wooden stilts and dance
And thereby sing to the loftiest casements.
See how with polish I bow from the waist.
Space for these stilts! More space or I fail!

And a crown I say for my buffoon's head.
Yet no more fool am I than King Canute,
Lord of our tribe, who scanned and scorned;
Who half-deceived, believed; and, poet, missed
The first white waves come nuzzling at his feet;
Then damned the courtiers and the foolish trial
With a most bewildering and unkingly jest.

It was the mist. It lies inside one like a destiny.
A real Jonah it lies rotting like a lung.
And I know myself undone who am a clown
And wear a wreath of mist for a crown;
Mist with the scent of dead apples,
Mist swirling from black oily waters at evening,
Mist from the fraternal graves of cemeteries.

It shall drive me to beg my food and at last
Hurl me broken I know and prostrate on the road;
Like a huge toad I saw, entire but dead,

That Time mordantly had blacked; O pressed
To the moist earth it pled for entry.
I shall be I say that stiff toad for sick with mist
And crazed I smell the odour of mortality.

And Time flames like a paraffin stove
And what it burns are the minutes I live.
At certain middays I have watched the cars
Bring me from afar their windshield suns;
What lay to my hand were blue fenders,
The suns extinguished, the drivers wearing sunglasses.
And it made me think I had touched a hearse.

So whatever else poetry is freedom. Let
Far off the impatient cadences reveal
A padding for my breathless stilts. Swivel,
O hero, in the fleshy groves, skin and glycerine,
And sing of lust, the sun's accompanying shadow
Like a vampire's wing, the stillness in dead feet –
Your stave brings resurrection, O aggrievèd king.

BERRY PICKING

Silently my wife walks on the still wet furze
Now darkgreen the leaves are full of metaphors
Now lit up is each tiny lamp of blueberry.
The white nails of rain have dropped and the sun is free.

And whether she bends or straightens to each bush
To find the children's laughter among the leaves
Her quiet hands seem to make the quiet summer hush –
Berries or children, patient she is with these.

I only vex and perplex her; madness, rage
Are endearing perhaps put down upon the page;
Even silence daylong and sullen can then
Enamour as restraint or classic discipline.

So I envy the berries she puts in her mouth,
The red and succulent juice that stains her lips;
I shall never taste that good to her, nor will they
Displease her with a thousand barbarous jests.

How they lie easily for her hand to take,
Part of the unoffending world that is hers;
Here beyond complexity she stands and stares
And leans her marvellous head as if for answers.

No more the easy soul my childish craft deceives
Nor the simpler one for whom yes is always yes;
No, now her voice comes to me from a far way off
Though her lips are redder than the raspberries.

CAIN

Taking the air rifle from my son's hand,
I measured back five paces, the Hebrew
In me, narcissist, father of children,
Laid to rest. From there I took aim and fired.
The silent ball hit the frog's back an inch
Below the head. He jumped at the surprise
Of it, suddenly tickled or startled
(He must have thought) and leaped from the wet sand
Into the surrounding brown water. But
The ball had done its mischief. His next spring
Was a miserable flop, the thrust all gone
Out of his legs. He tried – like Bruce – again,
Throwing out his sensitive pianist's
Hands as a dwarf might or a helpless child.
His splash disturbed the quiet pondwater
And one old frog behind his weedy moat
Blinking, looking self-complacently on.
The lin's surface at once became closing
Eyelids and bubbles like notes of music

Liquid, luminous, dropping from the page
White, white-bearded, a rapid crescendo
Of inaudible sounds and a crones' whispering
Backstage among the reeds and bulrushes
As for an expiring Lear or Oedipus.

But Death makes us all look ridiculous.
Consider this frog (dog, hog, what you will)
Sprawling, his absurd corpse rocked by the tides
That his last vain spring had set in movement.
Like a retired oldster, I couldn't help sneer,
Living off the last of his insurance:
Billows – now crumbling – the premiums paid.
Absurd, how absurd. I wanted to kill
At the mockery of it, kill and kill
Again – the self-infatuate frog, dog, hog,
Anything with the stir of life in it,
Seeing the dead leaper, Chaplin-footed,
Rocked and cradled in this afternoon
Of tranquil water, reeds, and blazing sun,
The hole in his back clearly visible
And the torn skin a blob of shadow
Moving when the quiet poolwater moved.
O Egypt, marbled Greece, resplendent Rome,
Did you also finally perish from a small bore
In your back you could not scratch? And would
Your mouths open ghostily, gasping out
Among the murky reeds, the hidden frogs,
We climb with crushed spines toward the heavens?

When the next morning I came the same way
The frog was on his back, one delicate
Hand on his belly, and his white shirt front
Spotless. He looked as if he might have been
A comic; tapdancer apologizing
For a fall, or an Emcee, his wide grin
Coaxing a laugh from us for an aside
Or perhaps a joke we didn't quite hear.

PAGING MR. SUPERMAN

I myself walked into the Sheraton
And after remarking his raw nose
Was part natal umbilicus I told
The clerk in the loudest voice I could bear:
"Page me Mr. Superman." He looked
Diffidently at me but acceding
My tie-pin, made of the rarest onyx,
Belonged to neither a sour fanatic
Nor one sick in the head from eating
Shrimps canned in the Andes and contraband
Here, he signalled for a call boy who came
Running all spongy with awareness,
His cheeks flapping in the air-conditioned
Air and his white dentures extended in
Warmest greeting. "Page Mr. Superman,"
The uneasy clerk said eyeing my pin
To re-assure himself and in his mind
Recapitulating the small number
Of paid two-week vacations he had had.
Luckily the grey-haired call boy was one
Of the ignatzes the cities now breed
Reliably and with a more exact
Efficiency than former days.
                                        He saw
Nothing remarkable in the clerk's request
And sent his voice through the loudspeaker
Of his imagination constructed
In the faraway days of childhood in rooms
Alone with Atlas and the last pages
Of boys' magazines. I heard the glory
Of it that afternoon like the closing
Chords of Handel's Messiah. "Superman"
It rang out clear across the floor polish.

"Mr. Superman." There was such triumph,
Such wildest exultation in his voice,
The pale cigarette girl at the counter
For the first time in her life gave wrong change
And all the elevators raced upwards
As if a pistol shot had startled them;
They did not stop till they had crashed the roof
Where one can see their solemn closed cages
Side by side and standing pigeon-spotted
Like the abunas on the cathedral
Dazed-seeming by the wildest flight of all.

This was the cocktail hour when love
Is poured over ice-cubes and executives
Lay their shrewdest plans for the birth of twins
With silver spoons; when one forgets the ships
Aground in fog, the pilot with letters
For mountain peaks and snow; the silent poor;
Or the wife with pre-menstrual tensions;
When Asia is rubbed out with an olive,
A truce ordered to the day's massacres.
I saw only six in the large lobby,
Five men and one solitary woman,
Who hearing Mr. Superman called
Looked up at once from the puddle of their
Lives where they stood at the edges making
Crumbling mud pies out of paper money.
While the stout woman adjusted her bra
And studied the door of the Gents' Room,
The men had risen to their feet watching
Scared and breathless the quick revolving door
As if they expected the flashing blades
To churn him into visible substance.
But no one emerged from either place;
The unusual name was finally

Lost under the carpet where it was found
The next day badly deteriorated.
The condemned six returned to their postures
And the hour rained down the familiar
Wrinkles and the smiles cutting like glass.
The call boy gave it as his verdict
Superman was nowhere in the lobby,
And the tall clerk now regarding my pin
Mistrustfully rubbed the umbilical
Part of his nose that was raw and itchy.
"He has not yet arrived," he said. "Perhaps
He'll come later." For a split second
I thought he was making game of me
But his eyes were steady as if fixed
On a T.V. serial. I thanked him
And smiling amiably in all
Directions of the bell-shaped womb, I walked
Out into the ordinary sunshine.

CÔTE DES NEIGES CEMETERY

As if it were a faultless poem, the odour
Is both sensuous and intellectual,
And of faded onion peel its colour;
For here the wasting mausoleums brawl
With Time, heedless and mute; their voice
Kept down, polite yet querulous –
Assuredly courtesy must at last prevail.

Away from the markings of the poor
On slope and summit the statuary is vain
And senatorial (now the odour's
A high-pitched note, piercing the brain)
Where lying together are judge and barrister
And some whose busts look on a shrunk estate.

Persuade yourself it is a Warner set
Unreal and two-dimensional, a facade,
Though our mortal tongues are furred with death:
A ghost city where live autumn birds flit
And small squirrels dart from spray to spray
And this formal scene is a kind of poetry.

Especially the tomb of Moise Wong, alien
And quaint among French Catholic names
Or the drainage pipes inanimate and looped
You may conceive as monstrous worms.
Undying paradox! Yet, love, look again:
Like an insinuation of leaves in snow

And sad, sad with surrender are the tablets
For the Chinese nuns; or, a blade between, the rows
Exact as alms, of les Sourdes et Muettes
And of les Aveugles: – and this, dear girl,
Is the family plot of Père Loisel and his wife
Whose jumbled loins in amorous sweat
Spawned these five neat graves in a semicircle.

LAURENTIAN RHAPSODY

Tomorrow my little one will come.
She alone reckons me as I am:

Sensual, argumentative
(Only when sober) lazy and naïve.

And she's wise in other ways: she's neat
And her small body is fragrant sweet.

And it's a miracle one this young
Should have the mastery of her tongue.

She say she loves my distinguished ears
And I have likened her breasts to pears.

Well, she'll bring books, Bacardi rhum
And her own irreplaceable bum.

And I'll pretend I am Bliss Carman,
That tramp and terrible bohemian.

And Kit – but what native poetess
Was other than over-virtuous?

So to our own act: we sit near the stove;
When it grows too warm – why, we make love!

Should the paraffin fire die down
We skip out on love and zip to town.

Our game? She asks the bartenders there,
Do they know a sweetheart that's more fair.

Since they don't they must give Kit and me
A double glass of Irish whiskey.

Then off we zoom to the next village
To find a priest who can guess my age.

As much as he tries, he cannot tell.
His forfeit: he must ring his church bell.

Ring out to the cold Laurentian sky;
They sweep to the grave grey hair, bright eye.

O ring out, harsh bells, ring out my years:
In a young girl's arms there are no tears.

And they who smile, say the moral's old,
Had best apply it before they're cold.

Let's lose no time but make a fine feast.
Invite the bartenders and the priest.

Let them come, be merry for our sake
In this rented cabin by the lake.

The bartenders can't leave, they've business;
But the young priest will send his mistress.

And since you're fair and I am forty-six
We'll – forgive the rhyme – we'll teach her tricks.

And we'll make such noise the fish shall come
To lead us out in a moonlight swim.

On a rock the priest's girl will preside
While Beauty and Age swim side by side.

Bless the mistress, bless her young priest,
Bless my grey hairs and your lovely breast.

Bless the village, O bless this cabin,
And bless the waters where ends all sin. Amen.

FAMILY PORTRAIT

That owner of duplexes
has enough gold to sink himself
on a battleship. His children,
two sons and a daughter, are variations
on the original gleam: that is,
    slobs with a college education.

Right now the four of them
are seated in the hotel's dining-room
munching watermelons.

With the assurance of money
in the bank
they spit out the black, cool, elliptical
melonseeds, and you can tell
the old man has rocks
but no culture: he spits,
    gives the noise away free.

The daughter however is embarrassed
(Second Year Arts, McGill) and sucks harder
to forget.

They're about as useless
as tits on a bull,
and I think:
"Thank heaven I'm not
Jesus Christ —
I don't have to love them."

CLIMBING

Along the road I walk with my son
Noting the damp ferns, the confusion
Of goldenrods, mulleins, chickories
That grow by the road's side. But he sees
A sandhill to the left and he's gone,
His high voice urging me, "Quick, come on!"
But he does not wait to see if I
Have reached him and his excited cry,
Nor does he care overmuch whether
The sand-dust from his quick feet cover
My head and neck, the face turned away.
There'd be no point shouting, "Hold, son. Stay."
He wouldn't hear me for all the noise
He makes: yet supposing he did what's
Gained asking a boy that's lithe-limbed
To stop midway an important climb?
So I let him go on till his feet
Are bravely planted on the summit.
From there of course he at once looks down;
He laughs when he sees my past concern.
How can I show him my relieved face
Is for more than a boy's morning race?
So I grin and wave up to him there
(This poet, lover, frail Balboa)
The goldenrod I hold in my hand,
While white sprays of dust still drift on
Forcing me to shade my eyes and frown.
But son capers on his hill of sand.

CAT DYING IN AUTUMN

I put the cat outside to die,
Laying her down
Into a rut of leaves
Cold and bloodsoaked;
Her moan
Coming now more quiet
And brief in October's economy
Till the jaws
Opened and shut on no sound.

Behind the wide pane
I watched the dying cat
Whose fur like a veil of air
The autumn wind stirred
Indifferently with the leaves;
Her form (or was it the wind?)
Still breathing –
A surprise of white.

And I was thinking
Of melting snow in spring
Or a strip of gauze
When a sparrow
Dropped down beside it
Leaning his clean beak
Into the hollow;
Then whirred away, his wings,
You may suppose, shuddering.

Letting me see
From my house
The twisted petal
That fell
Between the ruined paws
To hold or play with,
And the tight smile
Cats have for meeting death.

PARTING

What's the use if we should walk
Arm-about-the-waist and talk
Our married foolish hearts out;
Nor you rage, nor I shout
Out of grief, vexation
For the dusty road taken,
And that wound that's worst of all
Because unintelligible –
The passionate will to hurt;
And the recollected mirth,
And the intolerable pain
Of bright well-favoured children
Growing, fed on our evil,
Sullen, asymmetrical,
Their unformed unattached cry
Blood on our eardrums till we die:
For all that, troubled wisdom,
Experience and that dream
Of courage by which we live
Though the living be fictive,
Stony, a waste of breath,
And poor excuse for shunning death
Would make us give hands and part;
Reteach to cold lips an art
Of smiling they one time knew
Tender and lovely as the dew;
And drop from them a wry kiss
Into our growing emptiness,
Implanting there compassion
Beyond charity and reason
For the stubborn human fault
Brought from that fashionable vault
Men say floats invisibly
In a hollow of the sky,
But theologians reason well
For a thick basement in hell.
Yet it's the business of none

To say whether up or down;
Enough to know the human
As a mixed constitution
Imploring and fallible,
Choosing and despising ill;
Enough that we two can find
A laughter in the mind
For the interlocking grass
The winds part as they pass;
Or fallen on each other,
Leaf and uprooted flower.

FOR MAO TSE-TUNG: A MEDITATION ON FLIES AND KINGS

So, circling about my head, a fly.
Haloes of frantic monotone.
Then a smudge of blood smoking
On my fingers, let Jesus and Buddha cry.

Is theirs the way? Forgiveness of hurt?
Leprosariums? Perhaps. But I
Am burning flesh and bone,
An indifferent creature between
Cloud and a stone;
Smash insects with my boot,
Feast on torn flowers, deride
The nonillion bushes by the road
(Their patience is very great.)
Jivatma, they endure,
Endure and proliferate.

And the meek-browed and poor
In their solid tenements
(Etiolated, they do not dance.)
Worry of priest and of commissar:

None may re-create them who are
Lowly and universal as the moss
Or like vegetation the winds toss
Sweeping to the open lake and sky.
I put down these words in blood
And would not be misunderstood:
They have their Christs and their legends
And out of their pocks and ailments
Weave dear enchantments –
Poet and dictator, you are as alien as I.

On this remote and classic lake
Only the lapsing of the water can I hear
And the cold wind through the sumac.
The moneyed and their sunburnt children
Swarm other shores. Here is ecstasy,
The sun's outline made lucid
By each lacustral cloud
And man naked with mystery.
They dance best who dance with desire,
Who lifting feet of fire from fire
Weave before they lie down
A red carpet for the sun.

I pity the meek in their religious cages
And flee them; and flee
The universal sodality
Of joy-haters, joy-destroyers
(O Schiller, wine-drunk and silly!)
The sufferers and their thick rages;
Enter this tragic forest where the trees
Uprear as if for the graves of men,
All function and desire to offend
With themselves finally done;
And mark the dark pines farther on,
The sun's fires touching them at will,
Motionless like silent khans
Mourning serene and terrible
Their Lord entombed in the blazing hill.

MY FLESH COMFORTLESS

My flesh comfortless with insect bites, sweat,
I lie stretched out on my couch of grass;
Chipmunks break like flames from the bleak earth.

And the sun's golden scarabs on the surface
Are aimless, nameless, scintillant;
Unmoving, or darting into pools

Of dark, their brightness gone. But the frog sits
And stares at my writing hand, his eyes
A guttersnipe's, leering. Or lecherous

As though an underworld savvy swelled
Those heavy-lidded eyes, xanthic beads,
They're desolation's self-mockery,

Its golden silence! Vacancy expressed,
Stressed by unblinking eye, fulvid lid!
And this vile emptiness encloses

Makes me too its rapt pupil. I goggle
At the quiet leaper, wondering
Will he rise up slim fairytale prince

At the first thundercrack. Will flash reveal
The universal lover, my Jack
Of hearts? A royal maniac raving,

Whirlwind's tongue, desolation's lung? Or flung
At the edge of this drear pool – mansoul,
Privity of evil, world's wrong, dung;

A cry heard and unheard, merest bubble
Under the legs of sallow beetles?
O, Love, enclose me in your cold bead

O lift me like a vine-leaf on the vine;
In community of soil and sun
Let me not taste this desolation

But hear roar and pour of waters unseen
In mountains that parallel my road –
Sun vaulting gold against their brightest green!

I KNOW THE DARK AND HOVERING MOTH

For vilest emissary of death
I know the dark and hovering moth
Whose furred wings overwhelm the sun;
And the blind minnows that cannot swim.

Oh, a fat black moth was my first wife.
She sat her weight on my greenest leaf.
Another moth was so fair a prize,
Melted my manhood into her eyes.

William Blake spied the vanishing heel,
Made all the white stars in heaven reel.
I heard his wild, dismayèd shout.
Rib by rib Urizen lugged me out.

Now at early dawn, my heart with joy,
Like any carefree holiday boy
I look at the minnows in the pond
And catch and kill them: they make no sound.

Lovely Aviva, shall we crush moths?
Geldings stone till we're out of breath?
Wipe the minnows from the goat-god's brow?
He hears their screams; he rejoices now.

For sun throbs with sexual energy;
The meadows bathe in it, each tall tree.
The sweet dark graves give up their dead.
Love buries the stale fish in their stead.

From crows we'll brew a cunning leaven;
From harsh nettles: lock them in a poem.
The virtuous reading it at once
Will change into rimed and sapless stumps.

My proud Love we'll water them, embrace
Over their unleaving wretchedness:
Till snakes cavort in gardens and sing
Melic praises for each mortal thing;

And from Lethean pond beneath a scarp
There rush the vigorous hunting carp
At whose gorping jaws and obscene mouths
Flit the vulnerable black-winged moths;

Poets, each the resurrected Christ,
Move like red butterflies through the mist
To where the shafts, the sloping shafts of Hell,
The globed sun enclose like a genital.

WOMEN OF ROME

The most beautiful women in the world
        Go past the Piazza Venezia.
Relics of the Risorgimento are stored there
Gathering the tourists' purchased stare.
They might gather dust for all I care.

Benito, Benito, where are your bones and thugs?

City of Caesars and Popes,
        Rome's imperial statues split and crumble.
Time and the rains that called their bluff
Have stood them there useless and formal.
My friend who knows the clever dupes we are
        Would call it elementary stuff
Sticking one's image in a public square.
Still, it worked. Look at Caius' metal finger
        Pointing to – where?

Italia, Italia, land without a recent past.
        There was a time when all went suddenly black:
How should you remember it? But that Roman girl
With the voluptuous neck and back
Is real enough in a shifting world.
I'd like to lie with her in vineyards plucking
        Grapes for her under the sun;
Or lie in orchards and pluck oranges.
I'd go on plucking and plucking.

Or that beautiful lady crossing the square
        Who once lent her eyes to Raphael, da Vinci:
The fountains of the city flying
Upward in the illusive act of dying
Shaped the dark rondure of her body.
        I'd follow her to the Via Ostiense where
Perched on a pyramid Death, the arch-romantic,
        Holds court among tombs and sarcophagi
Conferring on prince and pastyface alike a tragic air.

Cities and skylarks perish, molluscs on a column:
        Her loveliness will never die.
Beside an English poet's grave, fertile
With sunlight, we'd there embrace
        Or any other convenient place;
Kicking, if needed, epitaphs out of the way
        – Stanzas of dejection.
The agonized stance, beloved of schoolmistresses,
        Is out of fashion and of another day.

Among ruins and travellers' cheques
    Stay always lovely, my Italian lady;
Though tomorrow the heart of Jesus
Bleeds into a garish night
Where St. Peter's keys blink green and red
    And the mad bicyclists are everywhere.
In the pale palazzos of my mind
Dance on a marble terrace floor
    Lie down on my ghostly mental bed.

BECAUSE MY CALLING IS SUCH

Because my calling is such
I lose myself whole days
In some foul cistern or ditch,
How should mere woman's love reach
Across the lampless silence
For the sake of that craze
Made blind Homer dance –

I, crouched in the rainless air
And choking with the dust?
Yet so bowed, the readier
To kiss your palm, my finger
Touching your fabulous face
Beyond all error and lust
In all that dark place.

For the trove of images
One gathers in the dark,
The dark that's piled with refuse
I shall not curse the bright phrase,
Coronal of my eclipse;
Though had you wed a clerk
He'd have your red lips.

Not driven like a lazar
From his house and children,
His embraces as he were
Frog on your white sheets, my dear,
Made mock of and rejected:
Who'd turn had you chosen
A prince on your bed.

THE DAY AVIVA CAME TO PARIS

The day you came naked to Paris
The tourists returned home without their guidebooks,
The hunger in their cameras finally appeased.

Alone once more with their gargoyles, the Frenchmen
Marvelled at the imagination that had produced them
And once again invited terror into their apéritifs.
Death was no longer exiled to the cemeteries.

In their royal gardens where the fish die of old age,
They perused something else besides newspapers
– A volume perhaps by one of their famous writers.
They opened their hearts to let your tender smile defrost
    them;
Their livers filled with an unassuageable love of justice.
They became the atmosphere around them.

They learned to take money from Americans
Without a feeling of revulsion towards them;
And to think of themselves
As not excessively subtle or witty.
"Au diable with Voltaire," they muttered,
"Who was a national calamity.
Au diable with la République.
(A race of incurable petits bourgeois, the French
Are happiest under a horse under a man)

Au diable with la Monarchie!
We saw no goddesses during either folly;
Our bald-headed savants never had told us
Such a blaze of pubic hair anywhere existed."
And they ordered the grandson of Grandma Moses
To paint it large on the dome of le Sacré-Coeur.

My little one, as if under those painted skies
It was again 1848,
They leaped as one mad colossal Frenchman from their
    café Pernods
Shouting, "Vive l'Australienne!
Vive Layton who brought her among us!
Let us erect monuments of black porphyry to them!
Let us bury them in the Panthéon!"

(Pas si vite, messieurs; we are still alive)

And when, an undraped Jewish Venus,
You pointed to a child, a whole slum starving in her eyes,
Within earshot of the Tuileries,
The French who are crazy or catholic enough
To place, facing each other, two tableaux
– One for the Men of the Convention, and one puffing
    the Orators of the Restoration –
At once made a circle wide as the sky around you
While the Mayor of the 5th Arondissement
Addressed the milling millions of Frenchmen:

'See how shapely small her adorable ass is;
Of what an incredible pink rotundity each cheek.
A bas Merovingian and Valois!
A bas Charlemagne and Henri Quatre!
For all the adulations we have paid them
In our fabulous histoires
They cannot raise an erection between them. Ah,
For too long has the madness of love
Been explained to us by sensualists and curés.
A bas Stendhal! A bas Bossuet!

"Forever and forever, from this blazing hour
All Paris radiates from Aviva's nest of hair
– Delicate hatchery of profound delights –
From her ever-to-be-adored Arche de Triomphe!
All the languors of history
Take on meaning clear as a wineglass or the belch of an
        angel
Only if thought of as rushing
On the wings of a rhinoceros towards this absorbing event.
Voyeurs, voyez! The moisture of her delicate instep
Is a pool of love
Into which sheathed in candy paper
Anaesthetized politicians drop from the skies!"
(Word jugglery of course, my Sweet; but the French love it
– Mistake it in fact for poetry)

And the applaudissements and bravos
Bombinating along the Boulevard Saint-Germain
Made the poor docile Seine
Think our great Atlantic was upon it.
It overflowed with fright into the bookstalls
And sidewalk cafés.
Fifteen remaining Allemands with their cameras
Were flushed down the Rue Pigalle.

And when you were raised up
Into my hairy arms by the raving emotional crowds
Waving frenzied bottles of Beaujolais
And throwing the corks away ecstatically
(Not saving them!)
It was, my Love, my Darling,
As if someone had again ordered an advance
Upon the Bastille
Which we recalled joyously, face to face at last,
Had yielded after only a small token resistance.

THE CONVERTIBLE

Her breath already smelled of whiskey.
She lit a cigarette
And pointed to a flask in the glove compartment.
Then our mouths met.

She placed her hand on my groin;
She hadn't bothered to remove her wedding ring.
Her eyes closed with a sigh.
I was ready for the gathering.

You, Dulla, may prefer maidenheads;
But give me the bored young wives of Hampstead
Whose husbands provide them with smart convertibles
And who are reasonably well-read.

WITH THE MONEY I SPEND

With the money I spend on you
I could buy ice cream for Korean kings.
I could adopt a beggar
    and clothe him in scarlet and gold.
I could leave a legacy of dolls and roses
        to my grandchildren.
Why must you order expensive Turkish cigarettes?
And why do you drink only the most costly champagne?
The Leninists are marching on us.
Their eyes are inflamed with social justice.
Their mouths are contorted with the brotherhood of man.
Their fists are heavy with universal love.
They have not read a line of Mayakovsky's poems
    for twelve whole months.
The deprivation has made them desperate.

With staring eyeballs they hold off
   waiting for the ash from your cigarette to fall.
That is the signal.
When the ash crumbles, the man with the smallest forehead
   will smash a cracked hourglass, the sound
      amplified into a thousand manifestos.
Can you not see them? Can you not hear them?
Already they are closing in on us.
Your fragrant body means nothing to them.
Under your very eyes, velvet and remarkable,
   they intone that Beauty is not absolute.
They shout for an unobstructed view of your shoulders,
   your proud and beautiful head gone.
They will break your arms and slender legs
   into firewood.
The golden delicate hairs I have kissed
   into fire a thousand times
      will blaze more brightly;
But who will bend down to gather the flames
   into their mouth?
Who will follow their white light into eternity?

Because I love you better
   than artichokes and candles in the dark,
I shall speak to them.
Perhaps they will overlook your grace for my sake,
   ignore the offending perfection of your lips.
Perhaps, after all, you and I will start
   a mass conversion into elegance.
I will tell them my father made cheese
   and was humble and poor all his life,
And that his father before him turned ill
   at the mere sight of money;
And that a certain remote ancestor of mine
   never saw money at all,
      having been born blind.
On my mother's side, they were all failures.
Calliopes will sound for my undistinguished lineage

And the aroused Leninists will at once guess
    I am a fool in love, a simpleton,
        an ensnared and deranged proletarian
With no prospects but the wind which exposes
    my terrible hungers to them,
My counter-revolutionary appetite to be lost
    from all useful labour
        in your arms hair thighs navel;
And parting the clouds, one solitary star
    to show them where I am slain
Counting the gold coins
    for your Turkish cigarettes and costly champagne.

WHY I DON'T MAKE LOVE
TO THE FIRST LADY

Of course I could have her!

In a flash, with a snap of my fingers.

An arrogant magician,
I'd put words under her perfect feet
and make her fly to me.
She'd land in my arms
reciting one of my poems.
She'd remember nothing of the White House
except what I told her.
To draw from her one of her exultant smiles
I'd persuade her my lips
were official Washington.

Pah, I'm a degenerate poet
with a sense of honour!

I shall not take her.

Not while serene contractors
build kindergartens
for robots and goons,
and skinny Caribs
with beards sprouting from machine-guns
clamour
for blood, education, and cheaper roulette;
or the Chinese have a leader
who writes flawless verse.

President Kennedy does not write verse.

Not while Africa
explodes in the corridors of the U.N.

Lumumba, Kasavubu: a
D'Oyly Carte of exotic names;
but the drums,
East & West,
thwack unearthly rhythms,
and the opera-loving Congolese
lie much too still
on their dead faces.

A President
must stay up night after night
deliberating such matters:

My lovely, unlucky Jacqueline!

Still, when a husband
is so harassed,
shall I add to his burdens
by running off with his attractive wife?

Not I, not Irving Layton.

I'll wait until
the international situation has cleared.
After that it's every poet for himself.

SAGEBRUSH CLASSIC

And letting fall, "All life's a gamble,"
I assailed the desert's lush casinos
With craps, blackjack, and even keno.
Swift slung it: civilization is faecal.
So take a flyer. Which I did. Fickle
Or foolish one's luck; though I'd poems to show,
Was tanned-handsome, my movement deft and slow,
Some bunko artist raked my dimes and nickels.
All's shit. Luther protesting from a can,
Down-to-earth dealer dealing twenty-one,
Who clued me into a richer idiom;
Result? I can curse better. Caliban,
Roll those bones. At the end comes fuckface death
– Shows a pair of goose eyes on a green cloth.

DANS LE JARDIN

Dearest girl, my hands are too fond of flesh
For me to speak to you; and you are too tall
For me to think you beautiful, though beautiful
You are. You are some other's fortunate wish

Though alone and your idle limbs inviting.
If I should call to you, give you this verse
And later caress your thighs with these fingers
You would rise like a wraith, like some wan Viking

Come from the North, mists upon her shoulders.
Your eyes are too grave and too luminous
And pledge but one cold nocturnal kiss,
Their gaze putting out the fires that it stirs

Till I hear bells, a slowly dying sound,
Where no bells are; how then should I suppose
You passionately flinging off skirt and blouse
And letting my squat body pin you to the ground?

So as you move your blanket and thin buttocks
To catch the failing sunlight on your face,
I watch you from my stationary place,
My limbs as immovable as these planted rocks

And think of Fate and of your immoderate height
And of your spoiling gauntness; and of what blind
Excuse to make the ceremonious stars who'll find
Our bodies uncoupled by the coming night.

KEINE LAZAROVITCH
1870-1959

When I saw my mother's head on the cold pillow,
Her white waterfalling hair in the cheeks' hollows,
I thought, quietly circling my grief, of how
She had loved God but cursed extravagantly his creatures.

For her final mouth was not water but a curse,
A small black hole, a black rent in the universe,
Which damned the green earth, stars and trees in its stillness
And the inescapable lousiness of growing old.

And I record she was comfortless, vituperative,
Ignorant, glad, and much else besides; I believe
She endlessly praised her black eyebrows, their thick weave,
Till plagiarizing Death leaned down and took them for his
    mould.

And spoiled a dignity I shall not again find,
And the fury of her stubborn limited mind;
Now none will shake her amber beads and call God blind,
Or wear them upon a breast so radiantly.

O fierce she was, mean and unaccommodating;
But I think now of the toss of her gold earrings,
Their proud carnal assertion, and her youngest sings
While all the rivers of her red veins move into the sea.

NO WILD DOG

I tell my class
What man can do
No cobra can
And no wild dog

Or other kinds
Of vicious beast:
The prowling wolf
And the mongoose.

I'm told they hate
The smell of gas
And run from fires;
But that's not it

No, that's not it.
It takes reason
And spirit too
Which man alone

Evolved in time
So he can do
The amazing things
No cobra can

And no wild dog.

THIS MACHINE AGE

For fifteen cents
the label read,
the Virgin's halo
would light up
for three minutes.
The man dropped
the pieces of money
into the machine's slot
and looked about
the vast, gloomy church
empty except
for him and me.
When his gaze came back
to the halo
it was still unlit
– a dark infuriating zero.

He gave the machine
a careful kick
to bring the lights
of the circle out.
It didn't.
"Damn it!" he shouted,
"Why doesn't it light up?"
He kicked again
and muttered something
I didn't hear.
But I could guess
from the way he looked
he thought divine sereneness
a poker-faced fraud
and himself taken in
by the Mother of God.

WHOM I WRITE FOR

When reading me, I want you to feel
    as if I had ripped your skin off;
Or gouged out your eyes with my fingers;
Or scalped you, and afterwards burnt your hair
    in the staring sockets; having first filled them
with fluid from your son's lighter.
I want you to feel as if I had slammed
    your child's head against a spike;
And cut off your member and stuck it in your
    wife's mouth to smoke like a cigar.

For I do not write to improve your soul;
    or to make you feel better, or more humane;
Nor do I write to give you any new emotions;
Or to make you proud to be able to experience them
    or to recognize them in others.
I leave that to the fraternity of lying poets
    – no prophets, but toadies and trained seals!
How much evil there is in the best of them
    as their envy and impotence flower into poems
And their anality into love of man, into virtue:
Especially when they tell you, sensitively,
    what it feels like to be a potato.

I write for the young man, demented,
    who dropped the bomb on Hiroshima;
I write for Nasser and Ben Gurion;
For Krushchev and President Kennedy;
    for the Defence Secretary
voted forty-six billions for the extirpation
    of humans everywhere.
I write for the Polish officers machine-gunned
    in the Katyn forest;
I write for the gassed, burnt, tortured,
    and humiliated everywhere;
I write for Castro and tse-Tung, the only poets
    I ever learned anything from;

I write for Adolph Eichmann, compliant clerk
    to that madman, the human race;
For his devoted wife and loyal son.

Give me words fierce and jagged enough
    to tear your skin like shrapnel;
Hot and searing enough to fuse
    the flesh off your blackened skeleton;
Words with the sound of crunching bones or bursting
                eyeballs;
    or a nose being smashed with a gun butt;
Words with the soft plash of intestines
    falling out of your belly;
Or cruel and sad as the thought which tells you
                "This is the end"
And you feel Time oozing out of your veins
    and yourself becoming one with the weightless dark.

BUTTERFLY ON ROCK

The large yellow wings, black-fringed,
were motionless

They say the soul of a dead person
will settle like that on the still face

But I thought: the rock has borne this;
this butterfly is the rock's grace,
its most obstinate and secret desire
to be a thing alive made manifest

Forgot were the two shattered porcupines
I had seen die in the bleak forest.
Pain is unreal; death, an illusion:
There is no death in all the land,
I heard my voice cry;
And brought my hand down on the butterfly
And felt the rock move beneath my hand.

THE FOOL'S SONG

When I look back upon my life,
  What do I find?
  What do I find?
A single star, when I was seven,
That lit up earth and heaven;
  And here and there
  Some few wise and fair
But most, alas, unkind, unkind.

When I look back upon my days,
  What do I see?
  What do I see?
A thrush that sang from a windowsill,
Soul and ears to have their fill;
  But neighbours cried
  And my joy denied
And scared that bird, that bird, from me.

When I look back but yesterday –
  Ah, what befell?
  Ah, what befell?
A woman I told of bird and star,
Gleams and sounds that come from far;
  She brought me here
  Without sigh or tear
And bid me sing, but sing of hell.

THE CAGE

I turn away to hide my terror
Lest my unmanliness displease them
And maim for all a half-holiday
Begun so well, so auspiciously.
They are building the mythical cage
Whose slow rise allows janitors, whores,
And bank presidents to display love
To one another like a curious
Wound: the Elect to undertake feats
Of unusual virtue. Masons
Give stone and ironmongers, metal
As if these were forever useless
In a paradise of leaves and sun;
And a blacksmith, handsome and selfless,
Offers to blind me at once without
Charge. A quiet shiver of self-love,
Of self-approbation runs through each
At the discovery of so much
Altruism – unknown, hitherto,
Unsuspected – in their very midst.
The instance of the meek stonemasons,
The ironmongers and the selfless blacksmith
Seizes like a panic. Suddenly
Each one vies with his neighbor, avid
To seek out the more burdensome toil:
This one lugging spikes; that one, planks.
Affecting it is to watch their grace,
Their fine courtesies to each other
When they collide; or to imagine
Their tenderness in bed when they leave
The square littered with balloons and me
Blinded and raging in this huge cage.

A TALL MAN EXECUTES A JIG

I

So the man spread his blanket on the field
And watched the shafts of light between the tufts
And felt the sun push the grass towards him;
The noise he heard was that of whizzing flies,
The whistlings of some small imprudent birds,
And the ambiguous rumbles of cars
That made him look up at the sky, aware
Of the gnats that tilted against the wind
And in the sunlight turned to jigging motes.
Fruitflies he'd call them except there was no fruit
About, spoiling to hatch these glitterings,
These nervous dots for which the mind supplied
The closing sentences from Thucydides,
Or from Euclid having a savage nightmare.

II

Jig jig, jig jig. Like minuscule black links
Of a chain played with by some playful
Unapparent hand or the palpitant
Summer haze bored with the hour's stillness.
He felt the sting and tingle afterwards
Of those leaving their orthodox unrest,
Leaving their undulant excitation
To drop upon his sleeveless arm. The grass,
Even the wildflowers became black hairs
And himself a maddened speck among them.
Still the assaults of the small flies made him
Glad at last, until he saw purest joy
In their frantic jiggings under a hair,
So changed from those in the unrestraining air.

III

He stood up and felt himself enormous.
Felt as might Donatello over stone,
Or Plato, or as a man who has held
A loved and lovely woman in his arms
And feels his forehead touch the emptied sky
Where all antinomies flood into light.
Yet jig jig jig, the haloing black jots
Meshed with the wheeling fire of the sun:
Motion without meaning, disquietude
Without sense or purpose, ephemerides
That mottled the resting summer air till
Gusts swept them from his sight like wisps of smoke.
Yet they returned, bringing a bee who, seeing
But a tall man, left him for a marigold.

IV

He doffed his aureole of gnats and moved
Out of the field as the sun sank down,
A dying god upon the blood-red hills.
Ambition, pride, the ecstasy of sex,
And all circumstance of delight and grief,
That blood upon the mountain's side, that flood
Washed into a clear incredible pool
Below the ruddied peaks that pierced the sun.
He stood still and waited. If ever
The hour of revelation was come
It was now, here on the transfigured steep.
The sky darkened. Some birds chirped. Nothing else.
He thought the dying god had gone to sleep:
An Indian fakir on his mat of nails.

V

And on the summit of the asphalt road
Which stretched towards the fiery town, the man
Saw one hill raised like a hairy arm, dark
With pines and cedars against the stricken sun
— The arm of Moses or of Joshua.
He dropped his head and let fall the halo
Of mountains, purpling and silent as time,
To see temptation coiled before his feet:
A violated grass snake that lugged
Its intestine like a small red valise.
A cold-eyed skinflint it now was, and not
The manifest of that joyful wisdom,
The mirth and arrogant green flame of life;
Or earth's vivid tongue that flicked in praise of earth.

VI

And the man wept because pity was useless.
"Your jig's up; the flies come like kites," he said
And watched the grass snake crawl towards the hedge,
Convulsing and dragging into the dark
The satchel filled with curses for the earth,
For the odours of warm sedge, and the sun,
A blood-red organ in the dying sky.
Backwards it fell into a grassy ditch
Exposing its underside, white as milk,
And mocked by wisps of hay between its jaws;
And then it stiffened to its final length.
But though it opened its thin mouth to scream
A last silent scream that shook the black sky,
Adamant and fierce, the tall man did not curse.

Beside the rigid snake the man stretched out
In fellowship of death; he lay silent
And stiff in the heavy grass with eyes shut,
Inhaling the moist odours of the night
Through which his mind tunnelled with flicking tongue
Backwards to caves, mounds, and sunken ledges
And desolate cliffs where come only kites,
And where of perished badgers and racoons
The claws alone remain, gripping the earth.
Meanwhile the green snake crept upon the sky,
Huge, his mailed coat glittering with stars that made
The night bright, and blowing thin wreaths of cloud
Athwart the moon; and as the weary man
Stood up, coiled above his head, transforming all.

THERE WERE NO SIGNS

By walking I found out
Where I was going.

By intensely hating, how to love.
By loving, whom and what to love.

By grieving, how to laugh from the belly.

Out of infirmity, I have built strength.
Out of untruth, truth.
From hypocrisy, I weaved directness.

Almost now I know who I am.
Almost I have the boldness to be that man.

Another step
And I shall be where I started from.

A DEDICATION

Somewhere, alone in a rented room
a man is smoking a pipe under an orange lampshade.
His glasses, mirroring an empty wall, are blind;
the book under them has already declared bankruptcy.
Below his window, gabled roofs have put on their astrakhans
 for the winter.

A modern, complete with briefcase and fountain pens,
he's dogmatic as a parade sergeant though uncertain
whether the voice he's just attended to
was that of God or Satan's.
The church spire fronting him is of no help,
pointing in one direction only like a jammed compass
 needle;
and the wind's noise open to conflicting interpretations.
Like bankers radiant at convention tables
 the lights of the city blink their unconcern.

He only knows, this strange man,
that through dense Nothingness somehow he must open
a path to power and insight – to freedom
though he and his brief azure soon afterwards
be swallowed up in the night air for ever.
When all the lights are put out, the buildings darkened,
he blesses a snowflake – a solitary particle of light
expiring on the black fire escape
 and gladly dying in its death, lives.

Therefore I've written this poem for him.

EL CAUDILLO

In Spain,
Generalissimo Franco is top dog:
you know that
because in every village and town
there are at least
one *Avenida* and one *Calle*
named for him
– yet nobody speaks his name!
It's as if he didn't exist
but that some novelist
had given the alliterative title
– Generalissimo Francisco Franco –
to an obscure masterpiece
which no one reads any longer.
Still, it's this very silence
enveloping him
like the muteness believing Jews
offer their Tetragrammaton
that clinches the Caudillo's existence.
That, and the Civil Guards
wearing hats of shiny, black plastic
that hint at bull's horns.
At night, on the dark road to Denia
I saw one on a motorbike;
His back receding, the distance
made the contour of an idol's head;
and though I'm no bull worshipper,
remembering the obscene red mouth,
I can see how that grey apparition
out of the lightless groves of Crete
might turn a man's bones to water anywhere.

BALLAD OF THE OLD SPANIARD

"Old man," I said, "it must be a trouble
  To be bent as you are, nearly double.
  So bowed are you, your forehead scrapes your feet,
  Yet each day you parade along this street.

"Why are you not at home and in your chair
  With wife or son to give affection, care?
  What reason have you for disclaiming rest
  When to stay by your hearth is wise and best?"

Slowly he straightened himself on his stave
  And scowling, this passionate answer gave;
  Though he spoke, it's true, with so muffled sound
  His voice, I thought, must issue from the ground:

"You're not the first señor who on this street
  Has informed me my toe and forehead meet;
  Or bid me take my quiet rest at home
  And leave the bright streets for *chicos* to roam.

"I shall have a long time for my repose
  Where one's feet are kept away from one's nose;
  I say, before the eyes are shut; the tongue, mute
  One should be all fingers – the world, his fruit.

"Señor, I walked as though I wore a crown
  Till Time's bandilleros brought my head down;
  Yet I'm not bent with seeking for my grave:
  When I meet Death I'll strike him with this stave."

He raised his stick as though to strike at me;
  Then lowered it with Spanish courtesy,
  And putting one hand on his shrunken thigh
  With the other – stave aloft – waved good-bye.

There was a pain in my throat; in my eyes, mist
  For Death's frail, quixotic antagonist:
  This pair of scissors made of head and limb
  That cut, as he walked, the minutes left him.

PLAZA DE TOROS

I stand on a hill;
my mind reels in terraces
and I'm sucked into a whirlpool
of earth.
An evening wind rattles the almond trees.

In the hushed arena of the sky
the bloodied bull sinks down
with infinite majesty:
the stanchless blood fills the sea.

Triumphant matador, night
flings his black cape across the sky.

THE WORM

The filthy rain
blackens the street

Knowing that you lie
this afternoon
whimpering in another man's
arms

I picture you stretched out,
a stiffened corpse

And your cold vagina
extruding
a solitary pink
worm.

AT THE IGLESIA DE SACROMONTE

A death's head
from which falls away
a black soutane,
he conducts me
and the three withered nuns
from Pamplona
through his catacomb of horrors.

Complete with hairy lip
and decaying stumps of tooth,
the three withered nuns
from Pamplona
kiss relic and bloodstained bars
asking for intercession.

As they kneel and mumble
I hear reverberate
in cave and cell
the running bulls of Pamplona.

EL GUSANO

From the place where I was sitting
I watched the weary stone-splitters
Building a road to blot out the sun;
And seeing their sweating bodies
In the merciless, mid-day heat
I wished I could do it for them:
Turn it out like a light, I mean.
And I almost rose up to do so
When my eyes suddenly picked out
A strange, never-before-seen worm
Making its way on the dried leaves.
It had a rich, feudal colour,
Reddish-brown like the Spanish soil
And knew its way among the stones
So plentiful in Alicante.

I love lizards and toads; spiders, too
And all humped and skin-crinkled creatures
But most in love I am with worms.
These sages never ask to know
A man's revenue or profession;
And it's not at antecedents
Or at class that they draw their line
But will dine with impartial relish
On one who splits stones or sells fish
Or, if it comes to that, a prince
Or a generalissimo.
Bless the subversive, crawling dears
Who here are the sole underground
And keep alive in the country
The idea of democracy.
I gave it a mock-Falangist
Salute and it crawled away; or
Was it the stone-splitters frightened
The worm off and the brittle noise
Of almond-pickers? It vanished
Under a dusty dried-up leaf
For a restful snooze in the ground
But I imagine it now tunnelling
Its hard way to Andalusia
Faithful to the colourful soil
Under the villas and motels
Of those whose bankers let them stow
Ancient distinctions and treasure
In the rear of their foreign cars.
O plundered, sold-out, and lovely
Shore of the Mediterranean:
This worm shall knit the scattered plots
Of your traduced, dismembered land;
And co-worker of wave and wind,
Proud, untiring apostle to
The fragrant and enduring dust,
Carry its political news
To Castile and to Aragon.

PORTRAIT OF A GENIUS

My friend Leonardo
gives himself real scars
with imaginary razors
that he tests on the pubic hairs
of his old nurse.
When the storewindows of the supermarkets
are unwilling to listen
he shows me his scars
and we use them to play Noughts and Crosses,
taking turns winning.
Nevertheless he's always one game ahead of me.

I know he has two or three corpses somewhere
but I'm much too proud or cautious
to ask him where he keeps them hidden.
When I follow my nose
it leads to the cold green glitter of his eyes
impassively watching the massacre of a city.
If I question him
he shows me they are only boys and girls
playing in the snow.
Those are red scarves on the snow . . .
The time of day is sunset . . .
When the noise gets too loud
he turns off his Hi-Fi
and crawls under the bed
to stare at himself in the mirror.
It reflects only his boyhood teeth.
He tells me he will deed it to the world
if the Secretary of the UN
promises to polish it each day.
Still, he's wary of the UN,
finding the initials inauspicious.

My friend Leonardo
seduces women with words
and vice versa.
When he can't tell one from the other
he changes them both into his mother
who plays Noughts and Crosses with him
with carefully blindfolded eyes.
She always loses because she cheats:
he always keeps an X in reserve
to mark the spot where the game first began.

The day he discovered the spot
changes places when the sky is below
a certain temperature
he fired a bullet into his father's grave,
splintering the decayed coffin
into two elegant heaps of ash.
He often dreams of them now,
but it's hopeless telling him what he sees
is the atomic dirt under his fingernails.
He says he'd like to deed them also
to the world
but he's afraid that after he's been buried
in his father's stained shroud
they'll keep on growing
and wipe away the boyhood smile,
leaving only the blank terror staring from the wall.

INVENTION

The water from the sprinkler
has invented the three-leaf clovers
to hoard its pearls in;
the birds with their sharp cries and whistles
have called up the palmtrees from the ground
and made a present of them to the sun;
they fly over their waving tops all day long
like overseers of South American plantations;
buildings and statues
have asked a city to flower out of marsh and stone
and given it fountains where kneeling
with young girls it kisses its sleepy reflection;
the red lounge chairs have invented the green park
and the rich the beggars on the quay
whose tatters fluttering like colorful mediaeval pennons
assemble the hungry pigeons for crumbs
the silent apartment windows toss at them
before closing for ever

And the poem has invented me
to pry it loose from time's lockjaw
and from the earth that is dumb unless I speak
and the wombs of women
barren without the echoes of my voice

Away from the poem that is writing me
the world loses mystery and coherence;
and how inglorious and vain
are all words not in a poem;
like a bride's veil at the bottom
of a manila packing-case
like the shattered geometry of a bee-hive
or the crushed-open pod lying beside its seed
like an unoccupied chair in a park
like brown grass without water
or trees without birds
or empty cisterns where no faces come

When my head is filled with a poem
it is a hand holding another hand in love
it is the womb filled with fruit
it is my little son's arms encircling my neck
it is the sun lighting up the pearls
of all the three-leaf clovers of the field
at a given signal of the sky
it is the beggar resting his head
on a found treasure-chest for pillow
it is the prophet vindicated in his own city
it is the confident sunflower awaiting the dawn
it is myself as I truly am

May time keep me worthy of the poem
that has written me since time began

RHINE BOAT TRIP

The castles on the Rhine
are all haunted
by the ghosts of Jewish mothers
looking for their ghostly children

And the clusters of grapes
in the sloping vineyards
are myriads of blinded eyes
staring at the blind sun

The tireless Lorelei
can never comb from their hair
the crimson beards
of murdered rabbis

However sweetly they sing
one hears only
the low wailing of cattle-cars
moving invisibly across the land

CLOCHARDS

Like wounded birds that fall from a height
in ever-decreasing circles
they've finally come to rest on benches
and in the doorways of old churches;
or like the pitiful leaves of autumn
a sudden wind shoves into a ditch
and passes over, they lie in the unwanted
intimacy of misfortune, only their sordid rags
the fluttering banners of their separate selves

And one wears a cross for an amulet,
his sole covering for the night;
and one wraps himself in a newspaper
which the wind will read for him
through the long, monotonous hours.
It is they who know the hours of the dark
when the auto's spurt and snort in the empty street
puts another stone under their troubled heads;
when the diamond stars appear close, close
and sometimes ungraspable and far away,
and the body weightless yet somehow full of cares

They sleep like flowers in the crevices of streets
whose ragged edges abrade and pain,
making them raise their innocent grizzled heads
through all the periods of the moon;
who like themselves outcast, a poor clochard,
owns the waning night which no one wants.
And in the dawn the birds whistling them awake,
they sleepily brush the dream's deposit
of cold dew from their tatters
while dismay like a thief enters their eyes
at the renewed clamour of appetite and sense
the night had promised them to still forever;
and rising from the grim doorway and bench
they move like birds towards the unwelcoming street
silent and unnoticed as death itself

MAHOGANY RED

Once, a single hair could bind me to you;
had you told me: 'Jump
from the tallest building'
I'd have raced up on three elevators
and come down on my skull;
from the land of wailing ghosts
I'd have mailed you a fragment of skullbone
initialled by other desperate men
who had despaired of ever pleasing their lovers.
Once, pleasure expanded in my phallus
like a thin, excruciating column of mercury;
when it exploded in my brain
it was like a movie I once saw
where the earth is grabbed by the sun
and fried black;
or another ice age arrived on snow
and I danced hot and bare and alone
on a lost glacier,
hairy mammoths circling around me.
Once, I was a galley-slave
lying stripped in all your fragrant ports;
a tickle in my groin
made your skin a torment to me,
and I dived into the dimples of your knees
when you stretched naked and sexy on your bed.
Godhead, the Marxist revolution, History
that is so full of tombs and tears,
I stuffed them all up your golden rectum
and sewed up their sole escape route
with frantic kisses sharper than needles.

Now, without any warning
you are a middle-aged woman
who has tinted her hair mahogany red;
one of your front teeth, I notice, is discoloured grey;

I notice, too, how often you say
'phony' and 'artificial'
and wonder each time if you're not projecting.
Yes, suddenly you are a woman
no different from other women;
a little less nasty perhaps,
a little less insincere,
less contemptuous of the male sex,
wistful and dissatisfied in your contempt,
still hankering for greatness, the dominant man,
his flowing locks all the spread-out sky you want;
unfair, conscienceless, your bag of woman's tricks close
      by,
hard beset, as women in all ages have been,
needing to make your way, to survive,
to be praised immoderately,
to be nibbled by a lover's amorous teeth,
to procreate . . .
vain of your seductive wiggle when you walk away
      from me,
of your perfect breasts displaying nipples
I wanted to devour
and die choking, their pink tips tickling my throat;
vain of the fiery pennant under your chin
pinned there by your latest lover.

The bulb in my brain
once ignited and kept aglow
by genital electricity
lies smashed to bits.
I look out at the world with cool, aware eyes;
I pick out the pieces of grey glass from my brain;
I hold them all in my trembling hand.
Only a god could put them together again
and make them light up with sexual ecstasy,
but he lies sewn up in your golden rectum
huddled beside History and the Marxist revolution.
It is sad to be an atheist,
sadder yet to be one with a limp phallus.

Who knows
maybe if I had swung and knocked out
your one discoloured tooth
I would still love you, your little girl's grin,
small gap in your jaw
(who knows, who knows)
and not have wanted to write
this bitter, inaccurate poem.

SPECULATORS

There is a speculator
in Canada
who buys up snow:
whole valleys and mountains
covered with it,
and forests of evergreens
that wear their white capes in winter
as if they were Sisters of Mercy
racing towards some disaster.
I've even seen him dicker
for an ice-floe somewhere in Alaska
merely questioning the seller
about possible cracks and fissures:
the size and exact location of the ice-floe
didn't matter.
He once told me he'd like to buy
the frigid air above the snow
but can't find anyone rich enough
to sell it to him;
when someone as enterprising as himself
offered to deliver
a million tons of the stuff
he put finger to nose
and shook his head:

the price was too high;
besides, what proof
could the vendor offer
that the air had pressed against the snow
long enough to make it consistently cold
at least to the extent of one mile
both in length and depth:
so the deal was off.

I asked him what he was going to do
with all the acres of snow
he had accumulated
and he said something about Fort Knox
and minting a new kind of snowflake
or selling it to a ski resort
at a special discount
if they raised the Swiss flag
on three of their most popular slopes.
Why the Swiss flag? I could never find out:
he didn't look Swiss; more like a Turk, I'd say.
It was when I saw him
looking at some ice-cubes
in a glass
which someone had just drained
of lemonade
and opening his Moroccan leather wallet
to extract his business card
that I decided
his ambition to corner the market
on ice and snow
had to be thwarted.
I threatened to pour
the hottest sands I owned
in the Gobi and Sahara deserts
if he acquired so much as another snowflake.
This made him furious
and we came to blows.

Now they let him make all the artificial ice
in the place
and I've been warned
never to let myself be seen by him
carrying electric pads
to those who need them
and certainly
never with a kettle of hot water
in my hand or a cloud of steam.

AN OLD NICOISE WHORE

The famous and rich, even the learned and wise,
    Singly or in pairs went to her dwelling
To press their civilized lips to her thighs
    Or learn at first hand her buttocks' swelling.

Of high-paying customers she had no lack
    And was herself now rich: so she implied.
Mostly she had made her pile while on her back
    But sometimes she had made it on the side.

Reich she read; of course the Viennese doctor.
    Lawrence – his poems and novels she devoured;
Kafka at the beginning almost rocked her
    But as she read him more she said he soured.

Swedish she spoke, French, Polish, fluent German;
    Had even picked up Hindi – who knows how?
In bed she had learned to moan and sigh in Russian
    Though its rhythms troubled her even now.

A nymphomaniac like Napoleon's sister
    She could exhaust a bull or stallion;
Bankers had kneeled before her crotch to kiss her
    And ex-princes, Spanish and Italian.

And all the amorous mayors of France-Sud
    Impelled by lust or by regional pride
Would drive their Renaults into her neighborhood,
    Ring her bell and troop happily inside.

And pimpled teen-agers whom priests and rabbis
    Had made gauche, fearful, prurient and blind
Prodded by Venus had sought her expert thighs:
    Ah, to these she was especially kind.

And having translated several Swinburne lines
    She kept the finest whips she could afford
To be, though most aristocrats brought their canes,
    Ready for some forgetful English lord.

We saw waves like athletes dash towards the shore
    Breaking it seemed from a line of green scum;
We saw the sun dying, and this aged whore
    Noted how it gave clouds a tinge of rhum.

Engaging was her mien, her voice low and sweet;
    Convent nuns might have envied her address.
She was touched by the bathers below her feet;
    I, by this vitality sprung from cess.

And as she spoke to me on the crowded quay
    And reminisced about her well-spent years
I mourned with her her shrivelled face and body
    And gave what no man had given her: tears.

ON THE QUAY WITH MY MOTHER'S GHOST

At the far curve of the basin
it is all beautiful, all magical
for the mist has silvered the luxury apartment buildings
into remote fairyland castles

Turrets, fluttering pennons
and the pale trees outlined sharply
under a cloudless blue-grey sky
pilgrims climbing towards some cathedral
I can imagine but cannot see

It is the silver haze
magical, transformative

O if only my mother were alive
that I might show it to her

Look, I would say to her
this is what I saw when I was a boy
this I daydreamed all day long
Now look,
just as I imagined it!
the gulls, the castles by the remote, forgotten shore,
the silver haze
– a fairyland into which my boyhood
went walking
in search of a trumpet that was never blown

Listen, listen, someone is blowing it now
and surely that's my captive boyhood
waving at us from behind that pennant,
each flutter erasing a year from my years

O happiness!

And so I sit all afternoon
my head turned towards enchantment,
imagining a superbly arrogant princess
in her jewelled gown
dreaming of me when she looks away from her turret;

while below my feet
glisten the well-oiled bodies of the sun-bathers
and from the commonplace air
a balloon or beach ball
occasionally descends on a hairy belly
or a sunglassed stare
which my mother's ghost remarks
even more sardonically
than I

PIGEONS

When it begins to drizzle
the pigeons fly to the boughs of trees
where they sit quietly,
pretending they are birds of doom:
wet crows in a charcoal illustration
for a Gothic fable.
Purest illusion!
for with the first beams of light
from a repentant sun
they shake wetness and theatricality
from their tails
to alight once more on grass or gravel
in a fussy search for food; pigeons
are always hungry;
or is it insatiable greed
makes them ceaselessly prod the earth
with their pointed beaks,
their ridiculous slender heads
sawing the world
into two equal and severe halves,
one for each suspicious miser's eye
to take notice of
and disapprove .

WESTMINSTER ABBEY

I entered Westminster Abbey

and walked through the maze of chapels
and stood below the stained glass windows
and strode past marble busts
of philanthropists and admirals
and trod over granite slabs covered with inscriptions
whose meaning was instantly clear to my alive eyes
and I expected the slabs to open like trapdoors
after I had read the inscriptions
the way garage doors open when the electric beam
      is cut
but the trapdoors did not fall open
and I did not see Eternity that afternoon

And there was a stink

and I saw the royal chapels, any number of them
from Edward the Confessor's on
where the kings and queens of England
lie reduced to piles of dust
and I touched the caskets
and concluded they were indeed strong enough
to prevent ashes from blowing away

And there was a stink

and I saw Queen Elizabeth's chapel
which also contains the queenly deposit
of her sister, Bloody Mary,
and I ruminated six inches from their sarcophagi
that between the two of them
these ladies had dispatched thousands
through the trapdoor that leads on to Eternity

And there was a stink

and I saw the pompous niche
the Earl of Buckingham, the favourite of James I,
some say his bum-boy,
had cosied up for himself and family

And there was a stink

and I saw statues of great orators and statesmen
whose devastating rhetoric
was heard only by themselves
for the crowds moved on dumbly
to stare at some other approved name

And there was a stink

and I saw the Poets' Corner
where a bust of John Dryden almost faces
that of the dunce he savaged with sarcasm and insult
and busts of Burns, Southey, Coleridge, Johnson
as well as a centrepiece
made from the imagined likeness of Wm. Shakespeare
and they looked even more vapid and silly than the rest

And there was a stink

and for the first time in my life
I saw clearly what was meant by the English
        Tradition
how it is a slice taken out of Death
and made homey and negotiable like currency
a way of increasing real estate values
by squeezing caskets, urns, busts, memorials
into every last available inch of space
and I also saw that this can go on for ever
as long as the supply of famous corpses doesn't
        run out

And there was a stink

and I saw how the Englishman
is not passionate and grand and mystical
about Death as the Spaniard is
but sentimental, prosaic, and therefore matter-of- factly
seeks to profit by its existence
as he does from lucky deposits of coal and iron
in his right little, tight little island

And there was a stink

and how shameful, I thought, how unfair
to the dead who after lives of guilt and evil
had earned their right to oblivion like everyone else
to be put on display for curious tourists
smelling of travellers' cheques
and floating their democratic banalities where the air
moulders and is heavy with pathos and death

And there was a stink

and how I wished for a conflagration to raze this place,
for a flood to wash into the oblivious sea
slabs of granite, urns, busts, and memorials
whose lettering only three-eyed monsters might decipher
while the smaller fry, for a lark,
played hide-and-seek among the open caskets,
pillars of ash rising by day and by night
and making lovely iridescent bubbles for them
to bounce off a tail or fin

And there was a wink

and I saw the practical English
had stationed pious policemen everywhere
to keep fire and flood out and Death in,

and I bent down to listen
to Thomas Hardy under my feet
who informed me in a low confidential whisper
that all the insurance documents
(since life is a tissue of ironic accidents)
on this curious indoor cemetery
this sprawling profit-making mausoleum
are religiously kept in some other vault
remote from here

Where there is no stink

FOR MUSIA'S GRANDCHILDREN

I write this poem
for your grandchildren
for they will know of your loveliness
only from hearsay,
from yellowing photographs
spread out on table and sofa
for a laugh.

When arrogant
with the lovely grace you gave their flesh
they regard your dear frail body pityingly,
your time-dishonoured cheeks
pallid and sunken
and those hands
that I have kissed a thousand times
mottled by age
and stroking a grey ringlet into place,
I want them suddenly
to see you as I saw you
– beautiful as the first bird at dawn.

Dearest love, tell them
that I, a crazed poet all his days
who made woman
his ceaseless study and delight,
begged but one boon
in this world of mournful beasts
that are almost human:
to live praising your marvellous eyes
mischief could make glisten
like winter pools at night
or appetite put a fine finish on.

THE SWEET LIGHT STRIKES MY EYES

The sweet light of heaven strikes my eyes,
strikes the oiled bodies lying small and sensual on the
       beach
  and the blue-grey water of the Mediterranean
as it unrolls itself wave after wave
   upon the shore in bolts of translucent silk.

Five children, five glorious cherubs
float on the waves, swirling and twirling on their inflated
       tubes;
  and their excited cries as they fall with the waves
   and rise
rise piercing and joyful above the clamorous spray
   that gives again and again its white huzzas to the
     city.

And I see how at each end of the long promenade
the white buildings drop from the hill's summit
   into the sea like a light, bright waterfall;
while jet planes curving with the bay's glittering margin
   sweep over me unerringly to their target below the
     sky.

On the beach the graceless scavenging pigeons
insert their grey, probing beaks between the stones
    or for my laughter, like Japanese warlords in a film,
accomplish an archaic ritual of courtship or war,
      the males fluffing out their neck feathers and
        strutting.

Surely a piece of Eden broke off and floated here
and I must look for the scratched names of Adam and
      Eve
    under that girl's thighs or use her fanned legs for
    compass;
surely suffering and evil are merest illusion
    when such colour and sounds overflow into eye and
    ear.

The waves push the long afternoon shadows before
      them;
wind, sun work against each other for my maximum
      pleasure,
    and the sails holding the serene fullness of a good
    poem
are blue and white. God, the sweet light strikes my
      eyes;
    I am transfigured and once again the world, the
    world is fair.

LOVE POEM WITH AN ODD TWIST

Knowing
          that for as long
as I love you
     I shall stay
                    merely a poet,
a babbler & word-spinner
     content to describe
or deride
          the bloody acts
of brave men
(Homer was my ancestor)
                    my self-revulsion
twisted into dagger
     or religious text
(which? let vanity
          or opportunity determine)
I've brought
          pistol
& black holster
     from an ex-Nazi.
                    For target
I've nailed
          a blown-up photo
of Nasser
          to an appletree
& each time I fire
     I shout, "I don't love
you": meaning
          you

LIKE A MOTHER DEMENTED

Like a mother demented nature caresses
her children before she chokes them to death;
she raises tall palmtrees and whirlwinds to crack them;
only by continually devouring herself does she endure.

Out of her immemorial dung come flowers and stars,
come gracious ladies with tiny troutbones between their
     teeth
or goose-fat on the tips of flirtatious tongues
– with animal perfumes on their cool adulterous wrists.

At a later hour, the gracious ladies fall into the earth
where graveworms nibble all day long on their delicate
     parts,
unaware how fallen breasts and vaginas once gave birth
to mediocre poetry, to ecstasies and sighs.

For you, my sweet, you and me, the human race entire
she invented to watch this tragic and strange affair
for who wishes to play Hamlet when the gallery is bare?
Mind, Mind was in the mind of that performer!

Now when lightning splits the high arrogant oaks
and mountains rise and fall; or lions and tigers prowl
or crippled poets run and win the coveted laurel:
man, her darling pervert, sees and notes it all.

But the cost, the cost of this ghastly privilege
is unendurable guilt that we dredge and dredge
as horrorstruck we find our condemned selves on the
     stage
beside her, nature's most murderous tool and accomplice.

Love, I kiss your navel and my X-ray eyes see
fisheyes wink in your dissolving entrails,
and when I write my lying poems know I am using
an anodyne from which the fastidious man recoils.

OIL SLICK ON THE RIVIERA

Cowboy in black shirt, black hat, black tie
it rides the waves bucking like a bronco
and will not be thrown.

Let them arch their backs and suddenly go limp;
let their white manes toss wildly,
the froth fall from their mouths; though their fury
is unspent and never-diminishing
it is useless. Nothing
will ever unseat this superb, imperturbable rider.

Or from here is it chimney smoke I see
wind and wave have deflected?
A wavering net strung out along the margin
of the bay
to catch bits of paper and wood, weeds and ferns?
Or is it a funereal graph
for the drownings of vessels and people at sea?

Ah, but the green waves are stubborn, unyielding;
yet no less is the oil slick:
cool as a commissar, dark and crafty as the Georgian
it bides its time, knowing that history will always
        pardon
whoever has the patience and will-power to only hang
        on.

MARCHÉ MUNICIPALE

In the empty market
    coolness spills out
from vineyards
    gathered in boxes of grapes;
the rumour of orchards,
and pears full of an indisputable dignity
that lie like jaundiced dowagers
    in their white wrappers
and from freshly washed tomatoes
that flash in the surrounding gloom
like the neon signs of lost American towns
you speed past on rainy nights
    on the way to nowhere.

It is a coolness
    making herrings smell more rank;
in which the ripe colour of bananas astounds;
potatoes, a visible skin affliction of air,
lie mute, lie sullen in their earthy bags;
and the slow mysterious decay of olives
    filling the deserted aisles
with its black sensual irony discomfits
the pragmatic vegetables in their stands,
    countermands
the imperial fiats of pineapples.

And the stillness is such
    that waits for iron weights or a box
to shatter; or a child hidden
in a cupboard expelling his breath
and saying, "Ah, Ah" making it appear
    silence had spoken;
or a film with no commentary
showing machine guns and rifles
    fallen out of

the huge blistered hands of destiny
sands are burying; even the muzzles
that with a last malevolent squint
    at the sun
sink into a darkness and silence
more vast, more final than Pharaoh's kingdom.

IF WHALES COULD THINK
ON CERTAIN HAPPY DAYS

As the whale surfaced
joyously,
water spouted from his head
in great jets of praise
for the silent, awesome
mystery
he beheld between sea and sky.

Thankfulness
filled his immense body
for his sense of well-being,
his being-at-oneness
with the universe
and he thought:
"Surely the Maker of Whales
made me for a purpose."

Just then the harpoon
slammed into his side
tearing a hole in it
as wide as the sky.

YET WHAT IF THE SURVIVORS

Yet what if the survivors had wished
to see their families all wiped out:
the hated, tyrannical father
red-necked and forever bullying;

The competitive older brothers
and scheming sisters, the feared rivals
that pushed one aside with kicks or smiles
to stand under the eyes of mother

Giving her gaze as to no other
– the lucky ticket with the right signs;
yet she too baffling the heart with hate,
numbing the ego with affection.

What if she revoked her love and frowned?
Capriciously cursed instead of blessed?
Or one had sought the warmth of her breast?
Ah, the mind, the mind's a dish of worms!

Herr Hitler, were you the tool, the hand
huge as hate that ended all their fears;
their sinister, most secretive wish
bristling on your clipped, absurd moustache?

And the indigo tattooed on arms
the exact number they would have slain
had they but means equal to desire?
Sad orangutans are men who know

They're killers, the knowledge siring guilt
only further killing can benumb;
and the ape that walks erect has made,
Schikelgruber, the whole world your tomb.

ELEGY FOR STRUL

Shall I be maliciously funny, Strul,
and say you look like a display of glassware
on crisp hospital sheets as white as yourself?
You who were once a barrel-chested
Mephistopheles
tempting a boy
to follow him down a pedlar's road
with adventure stories
of money and success;
a whoring, roaring bull of a man
that kicked up his heels
in my mother's kitchen
and filled our ears
with strange Balzacian tales
of priests and nuns:
better known in the villages, you boasted,
than Jesus himself
whose girls you fucked and afterwards tucked
a cheap medallion into their raw hands.

(But you were no cynic.
Life, you said, is a fuck, a feed, and a fart;
nor did terror make you a hypocrite.)

I hear sounds tumble out
from your cancered throat
and I bend down to your perishing mouth
to catch the dreadful whisper:
I lived like a fool, I am dying like one.
There are tears in my eyes
for you, Strul
– ogre of stinginess I once hated so much
but not now, lying there and dying.

(Where's the booming, unmalicious laugh
that belied the meanness
that made you run like a madman
switching off lights everywhere
and leaving your wife's guests in darkness?)

Now I see only your wasted physique
time and bugs have diminished
and the fantastic vitality
it once housed
ebbing into the surrounding space
minute by minute,
a mere pulse on the pillow . . .
a flutter . . .
and then you are still for ever,
only the wan tubes in your veins stirring
and catching the quiet light from the window.

FOR MY TWO SONS, MAX AND DAVID

The wandering Jew: the suffering Jew
The despoiled Jew: the beaten Jew
The Jew to burn: the Jew to gas
The Jew to humiliate
The cultured Jew: the sensitized exile gentiles with
    literary ambitions aspire to be
The alienated Jew cultivating his alienation like a rare
    flower: no gentile garden is complete without one of
    these bleeding hibisci
The Jew who sends Christian and Moslem theologians
    back to their seminaries and mosques for new argu-
    ments on the nature of the Divine Mercy
The Jew, old and sagacious, whom all speak well of:
    when not lusting for his passionate, dark-eyed
    daughters

The Jew whose helplessness stirs the heart and conscience of the Christian like the beggars outside his
churches
The Jew who can be justifiably murdered because he is
rich
The Jew who can be justifiably murdered because he is
poor
The Jew whose plight engenders profound self-search-
ings in certain philosophical gentlemen who cherish
him to the degree he inspires their shattering aperçus
into the quality of modern civilization, their noble
and eloquent thoughts on scapegoatism and un-
merited agony
The Jew who agitates the educated gentile, making him
pace back and forth in his spacious well-aired
library
The Jew who fills the authentic Christian with loathing
for himself and his fellow-Christians
The Jew no one can live with: he has seen too many
conquerors come and vanish, the destruction of
too many empires
The Jew in whose eyes can be read the doom of nations
even when he averts them in compassion and
disgust
The Jew every Christian hates, having shattered his
self-esteem and planted the seeds of doubts in his
soul
The Jew everyone seeks to destroy, having instilled self-
division in the heathen

Be none of these, my sons
My sons, be none of these
Be gunners in the Israeli Air Force

THE GRAVEYARD

Lord, I understand the plan, the news is out:
I kill him, he kills me, change and change about,
And you ever in the right; and no wonder
Since it's no great matter who's up, who's under.
Teuton or Slav, Arab or suffering Jew –
Nature, Justice, God – they are all one to you.
The lion breeds the lamb and the antelope
As evil breeds good; darkness, light; despair, hope.

And though your scheme confound theologians' wits
All come and go sired by the opposites;
And they decree: he who slays and he who's slain
Leave on your excellent world no crimson stain.
The tragic, warring creatures that here have breath
Are reconciled in the partnership of death;
And death's akin to art, and artists please
To the measure they have stilled the contraries.

Energy must crackle on a silent urn,
Nothing catch fire though Jerusalem burn,
And the lion poised on the poor bok to spring
Hold in his furious jaws no suffering.
Motion and rest, love and hate, heaven and hell
Here cease their Punch-and-Judy show: all is well.
There is no pain in the graveyard or the voice
Whispering to the tombstones: "Rejoice, rejoice."

INDEX OF TITLES

INDEX OF FIRST LINES